# 30-MINUTE MEALS

**HPBooks**®

## Susan Brown Draudt

With her degree in Home Economics from California State University, Los Angeles, Susan found opportunity for appliance-manufacturer demonstration work. From that beginning, Susan has significantly increased her involvement in the food industry. Her wide experience includes preparing consumer information materials, recipe development, product demonstrations and food photography. As an excellent teacher, Susan enjoys teaching cooking classes at department stores, cookware shops and cooking schools. She is also the author of *Food Processor Cookery,* published by HPBooks.

Susan's busy family life with husband Dennis and children, Danielle and Michael, leaves her little time to cook meals. As a result, she has developed a wide range of recipes that can be prepared in a short time. These recipes are substantial, tasty and attractive. Like you, Susan wants to feel good about preparing a meal. With this wide range of quick, easy-to-fix recipes, you can meet the daily needs of your family as well as plan and serve those fun parties and elegant evenings everyone enjoys.

# Contents

**ANOTHER BEST-SELLING VOLUME FROM HPBooks®**

Executive Editor: Rick Bailey
Editorial Director: Retha M. Davis
Art Director: Don Burton
Book Design: Dana Martin
Typography: Cindy Coatsworth & Michelle Claridge
Food Stylists: Mable Hoffman,
Susan Brown Draudt & Carol Peterson
Photography: George deGennaro Studios

Published by HPBooks®
P.O. Box 5367, Tucson, AZ 85703
602/888-2150
ISBN 0-89586-308-1
Library of Congress Catalog Card Number 84-80068
©1984 Fisher Publishing, Inc. Printed in the U.S.A.

# Basics for 30-Minute Meals

How often have you looked at beautiful pictures of food in a cookbook or magazine? You probably thought, "It sure looks interesting; I'd like to prepare that sometime," with the emphasis on *sometime*. In this book, you can read a recipe or look at a photo and know you can prepare it in 30 minutes or even less.

Organization is the best tool you can use for saving time. Start by planning your meal. Be objective about how much time you have. Prepare a grocery list. Double-check ingredients that you think you have on hand. Retracing your steps is a common waste of time.

When you are ready to start preparing the meal, assemble all needed ingredients and equipment. Clean and chop all vegetables and open all cans and packages at one time. Read recipes carefully to determine cooking and chilling times. Having all the recipes for one meal completed at the same time takes practice and organized timing. As you work, keep your kitchen work areas clean and uncluttered to avoid confusion. Keep a sink of hot soapy water ready to wash dishes as you work. It really saves time and makes you feel more organized.

You will find, throughout this book, that recipes are written to save time in every way possible. The more organized you and your kitchen are, the quicker you will be able to cook.

## QUICK & EFFICIENT

A dinner doesn't have to consist of meat, potatoes and salad. Breakfast can be more creative than bacon and eggs. What is important in any meal is that the combination of ingredients gives interesting taste and visual appeal as well as meets your daily nutritional needs. The current trend toward simple, light, fresh foods is one that makes good nutritional sense and makes grocery shopping and creating meals more interesting.

Fast-food preparation does not have to mean defrost and cook. Some techniques to make food preparation fast include:

- Shorten cooking time by cutting ingredients in small pieces.
- Serve muffins and mini-loaves in place of bread.
- Serve meals family-style instead of individual plates.
- Organize shopping and preparation so you can accomplish more.
- Prepare foods for more than one meal at a time, such as peeling extra vegetables and shredding cheese.

In a 30-minute meal, every dish is important. Each one is a star but should also be complementary to other dishes. You may want to use a recipe you are familiar with but change the sauce or seasoning to make it fit in with your menu plan. In so doing, you may create a new recipe and probably a new favorite. Dessert is not mandatory at any meal, but it is a nice finale. Desserts can be light and done quickly, depending on your menu. In each chapter, there are wide choices to use in creating new menus or use those supplied. With this book, you can develop the ability to quickly prepare a tasty and attractive meal and enjoy cooking it.

 Throughout the book, you will find a symbol and a number. This is your guide to approximately how long it should take you to prepare the specific recipe. To coordinate recipes for a complete meal, plan to start the recipe that takes the longest and work progressively toward the shorter, faster recipes. With good planning and coordination, you will be able to make a variety of 30-minute meals. ❧

# Timesavers

Recipes that take hours to prepare rarely taste or look like they took hours to prepare! In fact, you were supposed to take hours in the kitchen and make it look like, "Oh it was nothing. I just whipped it up."

Using fresh, tasty ingredients that are readily available makes all the difference in flavor and appearance. In some cases, you use prepared foods of the same quality you would prepare yourself, but they need only a short preparation time. These might include pasta, tortillas or croissants. By using some prepared foods, you can give the appearance of a well-planned, organized meal within a short time. Most importantly, these meals and recipes are not complicated to prepare so you can enjoy getting them ready to serve as much as you'll enjoy eating them.

Timesaving appliances also help in efficient meal production. Food processors can slice, shred, blend and puree faster than the best chefs. A blender is second in choice to a food processor for versatility. It can chop, puree and blend. Microwave ovens are the ultimate timesaver, usually decreasing cooking time by about 75 percent.

If you are not familiar with how to use these appliances to their maximum, review the owner's manuals and, if possible, take a class or two so you can become the master. Once you know what these machines can do, you'll feel at ease and confident in tackling recipes you may never have considered before.

## KITCHEN ORGANIZATION

Having a well-stocked kitchen with appropriate utensils in good working order is a good start toward saving time in the kitchen. Purchase utensils to fit your cooking needs. Here are some ideas to help get your kitchen organized.

● Keep utensils close to where they are generally used. Always return them to their proper place after use.

● Arrange stored equipment for easy use. Don't overstack equipment.

● Organize the refrigerator with staple items, such as milk, eggs, butter and condiments, always in the same place.

● Store pantry staple items in the same place, preferably near where they will be used.

● Store foods so they are easily visible. Turn labels toward the front, right-side up.

● Review your staple inventory periodically to see if you have all necessary items. Keep a current shopping list.

● Inventory your wine. Group together specific types of wine.

## INGREDIENTS

Next time you're shopping and see a fresh herb, such as basil, buy it. Then find a way to use it. You'll be delightfully surprised at how good it really tastes. Fresh herbs can be used in any recipe calling for dried herbs. Use 1 tablespoon fresh herbs for each 1 teaspoon dried herbs. Crushing or chopping herbs brings out the flavor. Try experimenting by substituting one herb for a different herb called for in the recipe.

Store fresh herbs tightly wrapped in a plastic bag or by putting the stem ends in a bowl of water and covering with plastic wrap. Then refrigerate. If you're not going to use the herbs within one week, wrap them tightly in plastic and freeze them. There is no need to defrost herbs before using; simply chop, measure and use.

No-cook foods can be interesting as well as perfect timesaves. Items like cheese, fruit and canned fish need little preparation and no cooking before serving. If time is short or the weather is too hot to cook, work miracles with no-cook foods.

Serve cheese with crackers and you have an appetizer or snack. Fruit and an assortment of cheeses can be a quick and classic dessert. Cheddar and Swiss are the most common cheeses, but explore the deli case or go to a good cheese store where you can taste before you buy. Try blue cheese with pears. Or serve Brie or Camembert with pumpernickel, peaches or pineapple. Port de Salut or flavored cream cheeses are good for dessert served with cantaloupe or honeydew melons or strawberries. Serve heartier cheeses, like

Cheddar, Muenster or Monterey Jack, with apples, pears or grapes to make delicious appetizers, snacks or desserts.

Most people enjoy fruit. Perfectly ripe and slightly chilled, you just can't beat fruit. It's refreshing and thirst quenching. For an appetizer, serve grape clusters with fresh cherries or tangerines. Be sure to have a small bowl for pits or peels. A breakfast with fresh berries on a bowl of ordinary cold cereal elevate it to a special meal. For dessert, fill a glass compote with blueberries topped with a light dusting of sugar. Serve it with a pitcher of cream.

Keep canned seafood, such as tuna, salmon or sardines, handy on a pantry shelf. When needed, blend with other ingredients to make salads, sandwich fillings and appetizers. This book will give you several ideas.

### GROCERY SHOPPING

Shopping for several meals at one time can be a big timesaver. When quickly shopping for only a few items, go to a store you are familiar with to avoid wasting time running down aisles looking for items. Here are a few timesavers for putting away groceries.

- Leave out items you will use immediately.
- Clean all produce at one time if it will be used within a couple days. Produce for later use should not be cleaned at this time. It tends to spoil faster after it's cleaned.
- Rewrap any meat you plan to freeze for longer than one week.
- Divide meat into serving portions. Wrap individual chops and steaks separately for faster defrosting. Shape ground meat in a doughnut shape for faster defrosting.
- Always defrost in the refrigerator or microwave, not at room temperature.

### PREPARATION

- Set out all ingredients before you begin working. Mentally check where utensils are.
- Peel, chop, slice and mince all items at one time.
- Open all cans at once.
- Use timesaving appliances when possible.
- Combine recipe steps when possible.
- Do steps ahead of time when possible.

### COOKING

- Broiling and stove-top cooking are usually faster than oven cooking. Cooking more than one item in the oven is often possible. A good median temperature is 350F (175C).
- For foods to be served chilled, keep them in the refrigerator until ready to use.
- Foods will heat faster if they start out at room temperature.
- Use flat, wide cooking utensils of the same capacity. For example, a soufflé cooked in a 1-1/2-quart flat baking dish will cook faster than if it were cooked in a 1-1/2-quart regular soufflé dish.
- Make muffins, biscuits or cupcakes instead of large cakes or loaves. Thicker, more dense foods take longer to cook.
- While you have something in the oven or simmering on the stove, work on another recipe.
- Start foods in ovenproof cookware on top of the stove. Then transfer to a preheated oven.
- Serve your food buffet- or family-style. Serving and arranging individual plates is time consuming.
- Bake or chill the dessert while eating the entree. That's another 30 to 45 minutes you saved! ❧

# Timesaving Equipment

## FOOD PROCESSOR

**Slicing Disc**—Use to slice fruit, vegetables or meat. Cold foods slice more evenly. Use light, constant pressure when pushing food through the feed tube. Be sure to pack the food tightly in the feed tube so it doesn't fall over sideways and result in an uneven slice. For a nice look, shop for fruits and vegetables that fit into the feed tube without trimming. For coleslaw or finely shredded lettuce, use the slicing disc rather than the shredding disc.

**Shredding Disc**—Use to shred cheese, vegetables or fruit. You will get longer, neater shreds of cheese if the cheese is chilled before you shred it. When shredding, use a gentle up-and-down pressure on the feed tube. Don't try to push the food through faster.

**Steel Knife Blade**—Use for chopping, mixing and pureeing. Especially useful for chopping hard cheese, such as Parmesan or Romano, which has been cut into 1-inch cubes. Chop to desired fineness. To prevent over-blending of ingredients, use an on/off motion several times. Check to see how well-blended the food is. When pureeing, turn the machine on and let it run until food is smooth. Food processors are excellent for making fresh breadcrumbs or cookie crumbs.

## FOOD-PROCESSOR TIPS

• Foods to be chopped should be cut into equal pieces. Cut in 1- to 2-inch chunks for a more even chop.

• Foods of the same texture will chop at the same rate. Don't try to chop soft and hard foods together because they will come out in uneven pieces.

• Fill the work bowl only 1/2 full when working with dry ingredients; fill 1/3 full when working with liquids.

## BLENDER

A blender speeds up jobs like chopping carrots or onions, but it can handle only a small amount at a time. When chopping solids, like cheese or carrots, turn the machine on, then gradually add foods through the opening in the lid. For chopping vegetables, add 1/2 cup liquid for a fine chop. Blenders are also excellent for making crumbs from bread, cookies or crackers. Pureeing fruits or vegetables or smoothing out lumpy gravy works well with a blender. For mixing drinks or other liquids, fill blender container up to 3/4 full. For chopping, fill container 1/4 to 1/2 full. Be sure to cut solid foods into 1- to 2-inch cubes. Blenders do not do a good job of whipping cream, beating egg whites or cake batters, mashing potatoes or chopping large amounts of meat.

## PRESSURE COOKER

Pressure cookers speed up cooking time. That is especially true for foods that normally require long cooking times, such as less-tender meats and large vegetable pieces or stews where flavors benefit from long, slow cooking. Foods that should have a crispy outside, like fried chicken, or meat that needs to be browned, can be fried in the bottom of the pressure cooker. Then, put the lid in place and cook the food. Foods that require the same cooking time may be combined in a pressure cooker. Desserts, such as custards and bread puddings, can be cooked in less time in a pressure cooker. Read your owner's manual completely before using a pressure cooker.

## MICROWAVE

When using a microwave oven, place food in a doughnut-shape arrangement with the thickest part toward the outside for best results.

**Vegetables**—Vegetables keep their bright

colors and have good nutrient retention when cooked in a microwave. Avoid over-cooking vegetables; they become chewy or tough. Cover the dish with a lid or plastic wrap for even, faster cooking. It also keeps vegetables from drying out. Leave a small vent or opening for steam to escape. Size, texture and beginning temperature of vegetables will determine total cooking time. Refer to your owner's manual, package directions or *Microwave Cookbook, The Complete Guide,* published by HPBooks, for cooking times.

**Beverages**—Heat your drinks in a pitcher, individual mugs or even paper cups. The larger the quantity you put in the microwave, the longer it takes. Often, it is just as fast to heat cocoa for a crowd in a large saucepan on the stove. You can easily reheat drinks that have cooled. Be sure the cups do not have gold, silver or metallic trim.

**Defrosting**—This is a convenient and timesaving way to use frozen foods. Refer to your owner's manual for directions and times for various foods.

**Seafood**—Seafood cooks very quickly in a microwave. Do not overcook. Covering is important to keep moisture in. Fish fillets are often uneven in thickness. When cooking, keep the thicker edge toward the outside of the cooking utensil.

**Beef, Ham, Pork & Poultry**—Tender meat cuts give best results, especially if they are even in thickness. A defrost cycle or using 50 percent power is best for thawing meat. It is also good for cooking ground beef. Precooked ham needs only to be reheated in the microwave. ⚘

---

## *Kitchen Equipment Hints*

- Keep food processor, microwave or other timesaving appliances in easy-to-use locations.
- Make sure you have a good preparation area for chopping and cutting. It should be well lighted and close to a trash can or sink.
- Keep often-used utensils handy; hang on a rack, stand in an open canister or arrange them in uncluttered drawers. Make sure items can be spotted and reached easily.
- It's useful to have two or more of commonly used utensils, such as whisks, rubber and metal spatulas, mixing spoons or wooden spoons.
- With knives, quality, not quantity, is important. A paring knife and chef's knife are the two most useful knives. Also handy are a boning knife and slicing knife. Keep a steel or ceramic sharpening tool handy. Knives should be sharpened frequently during heavy use.

# Food Inventory

To have a well-equipped kitchen, there are many items to consider as staples. These food items can be pulled from the pantry, refrigerator or freezer to put together a meal on short notice. These items are also those found most frequently in recipes in this book. Keeping them on hand will mean fewer trips to the grocery store. Choose those items that appeal to your taste or that may inspire you to try something new.

## PANTRY STORAGE

Store canned or boxed goods with the labels facing forward so you can identify them easily. Store cans only one or two deep and one or two high. Store like-items together and always in the same place for easy finding. Sort cupboards every six months. Use older items or impulse buys that take up valuable space. Also check cans for any bulging seams or tops. Be sure to throw them away. Store as much at eye level as possible. Change cupboards if necessary. I use my typical pantry to store dishes, and eye-level dish cupboards for pantry foods. Date items that do not have a use-by or expiration date on them.

Standard pantry items might include:

| | |
|---|---|
| Baking powder | Herbs & spices |
| Baking soda | including: |
| Brandy, sherry, | basil, chili powder, |
| vermouth | cinnamon sticks, |
| Buttermilk baking mix | curry, dill weed, |
| Canned fruits | ground cinnamon, |
| Canned green chilies | nutmeg, oregano, |
| Canned meats | tarragon |
| Canned tomatoes | Honey |
| Caviar | Jams |
| Chicken & beef broth | Liqueurs |
| Chocolate syrup | Maple syrup |
| Clam juice | Olive oil |
| Coffee and tea | Olives, pickles |
| Cornstarch | Pasta & rice |
| Crackers | Powdered cocoa |
| Dried fruits | Red or white wine |
| Dry and hot cereals | Semisweet and baking |
| Fresh onions, | chocolate |
| potatoes, garlic | Shredded coconut |

| | |
|---|---|
| Soy sauce | lemon extract |
| Tomato sauce, | Vegetable oil |
| tomato paste | Vinegars |
| Vanilla, almond & | Worcestershire sauce |

## REFRIGERATOR STORAGE

Standard refrigerator items might include:

| | |
|---|---|
| Butter and margarine | Lemons |
| Cheeses | Lettuce |
| Chili sauce | Mayonnaise |
| Cucumbers | Milk |
| Dairy sour cream | Mustards |
| Fresh and | Parsley |
| hard-cooked eggs | Pickles |
| Green onions | Tomatoes |
| Half & half or | Yogurt |
| whipping cream | |

## FREEZER STORAGE

Keep a list by type of food in the freezer: bread, meat, ice cream, vegetables and fruits. For each item, list date purchased, weight of food or servings contained, and possible uses. Rewrap meat items by wrapping foil around outside of original container. Use a good freezer pen to mark on the outside the contents, weight and date purchased.

Organize your freezer by storing like-items together. Sort out the freezer every three months. Use older items. If any meat has a small spot of freezer burn, cut it off. Use the meat immediately. Don't forget to subtract items from the inventory list as you use them. ❧

Standard freezer items might include:

| | |
|---|---|
| Berries | Packaged crab or |
| Bread, muffins, | shrimp |
| croissants, tortillas | Pound cake |
| (2 or 3 types) | Red and green |
| Chicken pieces | bell peppers |
| Fresh herbs: basil, | Sausage |
| oregano, cilantro, | Sweet butter |
| rosemary | Vegetables: peas, |
| Frozen puff pastry | spinach, broccoli, |
| Fruit juices | corn, cauliflower, |
| Ground beef | green beans |
| Ice cream | |
| Nuts | |

# Entertaining with 30-Minute Meals

Entertaining at home is much more fun than eating out! You control all the variables and, with a 30-minute meal, you can graciously visit with and enjoy your guests. There is no need to spend the whole day in the kitchen preparing, only to be unable to enjoy the fruits of your labor at party time.

Organization is the key to easy entertaining, no matter how many guests you have. First, plan your guest list. Then set the date and time. If you always have dinner parties, try a brunch. You can be very elegant or very casual using different recipes. With this in mind, plan your menu. Start with an appetizer or two, even if planning a brunch. Guests always arrive hungry. Serving food immediately is a good way to warm up the group and get the party off to a good start. Appetizers that preface a meal should be light and contrast with as well as complement the entree. You want your guests to look forward to the entree. Don't overdo the appetizers. Many a well-planned meal has been ruined by too many appetizers.

Be sure to anticipate the food preferences of your guests—from the calorie watcher to the health-food enthusiast. If possible, keep a file on guests as to likes and dislikes. You might also keep a file of menus and who attended what functions. This makes it easy when inviting people again. You can avoid repeating something they have already been served or be sure to serve their favorite.

Colorful, unique and imaginative food combinations help assure a great party. The main course could consist of an entree with one or two side dishes. One side dish might be an interesting bread that is quick to fix. Don't overdo it. Keep your time schedule in mind. Your guests will enjoy one or two dishes perfectly done instead of a buffet of dishes hastily put together and overwhelming to look at. In deciding what to serve, keep in mind the serving utensils you have, as well as plates, flatware and linens. If you're short on any of these, try some of the attractive plastic and paperware now available.

Clean-up should always be considered. You can hardly enjoy your own party knowing you have a stack of pots and pans to scrub. With the lovely selection of paperware and napkins available today, you might consider using paper for easy, quick clean-up. Casual elegance seems to be the best theme for today's entertaining.

Dessert is a highlight most guests look forward to. It's a good way to leave your guests with a positive impression. Just because the meal was prepared quickly, there's no need to disappoint your guests. Anything from Kahlúa Chocolate Mousse to Strawberry Grand Marnier Ice Cream is possible within your 30-minute schedule. Remember, if serving a rich entree, a light dessert, such as fruit and cheese, will be appreciated. If the entree is lighter, then pull out all the stops for a rich, luscious ending to a party. You will enjoy it as much as your guests.

# Wines & Liqueurs in 30-Minute Meals

## WINES

Cooking with wine will enhance food flavors. But remember, it doesn't automatically produce a gourmet meal. Wine is really only another flavoring ingredient, like garlic or herbs. There is nothing mysterious about using it. Here are some basic guidelines to acquaint you with the best uses of wine in cooking, and what flavors go well together.

Most importantly, use a good wine that you would consider drinking. Don't use a rare expensive wine or the remains from a bottle of wine that was capped and refrigerated two weeks ago. Use a good, economical, fresh wine. The true flavor of wine comes through in cooking. Stale wine will give a stale flavor. Heating wine during cooking evaporates the alcohol and leaves the flavor.

Use wine to *deglaze* a sauté pan. Pour a little wine into the pan. Stir over low heat to loosen the small bits of cooked food left in the bottom of the pan. Once this is done, you can continue making the sauce, and the flavor will be better.

Add a tablespoon of wine to soup before serving, or toss wine with a little added sugar in a bowl of fresh fruit for a light salad or dessert. If you are serving a vinaigrette salad dressing, substitute the wine you will be serving for the vinegar. This way, the vinegar flavor won't clash with the wine you are drinking.

If wine is being used to accent the flavors in a dish, add it in the beginning of the cooking process. You may even want to *reduce* the wine first to give a more concentrated flavor without diluting the flavor of the dish. To reduce a wine, boil it in a saucepan until reduced by about half. The alcohol evaporates first, then the water, leaving the flavor. This can be done to any liquid when you wish to intensify the flavor.

A basic rule to follow when cooking with wine is: red wine with red meat and white wine with fish, poultry or veal. Usually, a wine you would drink with a dish is the correct one to cook with. Remember, red wine will give a reddish appearance to food, so if that is undesirable, such as in a cream sauce, use a white wine. You may want to use a small amount of wine left in a bottle for cooking. Cork it and refrigerate until ready to use within one week.

Here are a few suggestions for wine combinations that taste best—but let your taste buds be your best guide.

Seafood—Dry white wine or vermouth

Beef—Red wine

Pork—Dry white wine

Ham—Port or Madeira

Lamb—Red wine

Poultry—Dry white wine, red wine, vermouth or dry sherry

Cheese dishes—Dry white wine or dry sherry

Egg dishes—Dry white wine

Cream soups—Dry white wine or dry sherry

Meat or vegetable soups—Red wine or dry sherry

Cream sauces—Dry white wine or dry sherry

Brown sauces—Red wine, port or dry sherry

Fruits—Sweet white wine, Reisling type

Dessert sauces—Port, sweet sherry or muscatel

Desserts—Sweet white wine, such as sauterne, champagne or sweet sherry

## LIQUEURS

A liqueur or cordial has a base made from spirits, such as brandy, rum, gin or whiskey. Then it is flavored with herbs, citrus peel, seeds, fruit or cream. All have varying levels of alcohol. In the U.S., a liqueur must sell at 50 to 80 proof, although some are as strong as 110 proof. They must contain 2-1/2 percent sugar; however the level may be as high as 35 percent.

Liqueurs, because of their sweet taste, are best served for, or with, dessert. In cooking, they can be used like wine—added at the beginning of a recipe for a more penetrating flavor or splashed over the final product. The flavor in liqueur is concentrated, so there is rarely a need for reducing it before cooking. Try some liqueur-flavored coffees or Grand Marnier Whipped Cream to familiarize yourself with cooking with liqueurs.

# Quick & Easy Garnishes

When you want your food to look special, try a quick food accent. Garnishes are important to give that final touch or a splash of color. It is an inexpensive way to add pizazz to an otherwise plain dish. Garnishes can be very simple. Develop a stock of eye-catching ideas you can add at the last minute. Then prepare them ahead of time.

Over-garnishing is as bad as not using any. Be selective. Garnishing should not interfere with ease of serving. One garnish on the plate is worth two on your lap or the floor. The extra seconds used for simple garnishing are well worth the time. Here are a few ideas.

• Accent a platter of meat with grape clusters, green or black olives, small flowerets of raw broccoli or cauliflower, or drained canned-pear halves filled with mint jelly. Kumquats make a beautiful garnish, too.

• Keep hard-cooked eggs on hand for gold-and-white slices on various dishes—salads, thick soups or casseroles. A wire egg-slicer is an inexpensive, timesaving gadget worth its storage space, but not absolutely essential.

• Make attractive green-and-white rings from zucchini or cucumber. Remove the center seed section with a knife; then slice. If you desire to make a chain, slice rings and carefully join like links of a chain.

• Thin lemon slices do wonders for a clear soup. Or, add small tofu cubes, called *bean curd,* or a dollop of sour cream dusted with paprika.

• Narrow cheese strips, crisscrossed on a hot, green vegetable immediately before serving, are quick to do and quite tasty.

• Accent a sandwich plate or platter with crisp, raw carrots, zucchini or turnips cut zig-zag fashion. Buy a simple tool, sometimes called a *French-fry cutter* or *scalloped cutter,* which has a zig-zag blade. Look for this tool in kitchen-equipment departments or some hardware stores. With it, you can create crinkle-cut or lattice effects in as little time as it takes to slice with a paring knife.

• A pressurized can of whipped topping is fun for creating instant rosettes or ribbon swirls on a fruit salad or dessert. Use pressurized cheese spread on salads or crackers.

• A tiny scoop of sherbet can add color and texture. Experiment using it on a variety of food, not only desserts.

• Shaved chocolate is elegant on an iced cake or pudding. It is easy to do with your vegetable peeler. Nuts, flaked coconut, candied fruit or sliced gumdrops top off desserts nicely, too.

• Green-onion fans are colorful and attractive. Cut onions in 3-inch pieces. Cut each end in about 1 inch, making several thin strips. Place in a bowl of ice water to fan out. ❧

For cucumber or zucchini chains, cut unpeeled vegetables in 1/8-inch slices. With the point of a knife, remove center seed section, leaving a 1/4-inch ring. Make a short cut through each ring. Interlock rings creating a chain. For color variety, insert yellow or orange rings of summer squash between green rings.

Garnish hot cooked vegetables with long, thin cheese strips.

For onion fans, cut green onions into 3-inch pieces. Cut each end in 1-inch strips. Place in ice water to fan out.

# *Time-Management Ideas*

### Breakfasts & Brunches
● Be realistic when planning your available time.
● Use variations of recipes you are familiar with.

### Lunches & Light Meals
● Use store-bought products where they can save time and are of the quality you would make yourself.
● Consider saving time versus saving money when time is important. Use deli-cooked roast beef for sandwiches rather than cooking the meat yourself, or purchase cheese shredded or sliced.

### Appetizers
● Look for foods that require only assembly without cooking, such as cheese or fresh vegetables.
● Keep your freezer and pantry well stocked. See page 9 for some suggested items.

### Salads or Vegetables
● Think in terms of how you can save time. Do the cucumbers really need peeling?

● Have items cleaned and chilled ahead of time, if possible.

### Breads
● Using the proper equipment makes cooking easier and faster.
● Make bread in small loaves for faster cooking.
● Make muffins, biscuits or cupcakes when possible. The thicker, more dense a food, the longer it takes to cook.

### Desserts
● Simple and elegant is better than too much or poor quality.
● Cool foods quickly by placing in a bowl over ice or in the freezer.
● Use the time while eating the appetizer or entree for the dessert to bake or chill.

### Beverages
● Bag and keep extra ice in your freezer when space is available.

# Menus

Time-consuming cooking has passed its prime! Light, fresh meals fit better in today's busy, health-conscious lifestyle. Combining foods that are tasty and attractive yet quick, makes good sense. These menus combine foods for total preparation in 30 minutes or less. If you're looking for a larger menu, select additional recipes to add to your 30-minute meal. Keep quick preparation foremost in your mind.

Although these menus are quick to prepare, they don't skimp on flavor or elegance. *Fast food* means *fast to prepare,* not something you simply buy and reheat. All of these recipes are appropriate for an easy 30-minute party menu.

Using fresh herbs adds considerable taste and fun to your cooking. If you're lucky, you have herbs growing in your garden or backyard. Otherwise, check your supermarket produce department. Parsley, cilantro, mint, gingerroot, fennel or anise, garlic and dill are regulars there. Packaged fresh herbs, such as basil, oregano and rosemary, are becoming more common in major supermarkets. Small pots of growing herbs are available at some supermarkets as well as at nurseries.

Streamline shopping by planning ahead for several meals. Do the shopping all at one time. It's also fun to shop at specialty stores and look for new and interesting ingredients. Many specialty stores have high-quality convenience items, such as fresh pasta or croissants. They are as good as what you would make, but save considerable time. These items are good to keep in your pantry for last-minute serving decisions.

Feel free to substitute ingredients with what you have on hand or can find fresh in the supermarket. Use your imagination, but be sure to keep preparation time in mind. Change seasonings to meet personal tastes. If you're not fond of oregano, don't ignore a recipe using it. Add an herb you like, or eliminate it. Salt is a matter of personal preference—add or subtract as you wish.

Fast food with fewer courses doesn't mean sparse-looking plates. Arrange foods so they are pleasing to the eye. Give thought to garnishes but use them sparingly. A lemon slice or dill sprig will look fresh and inviting. Making food look attractive doesn't take a lot of fussy preparation. Remember, the food you serve should always be the center of attention.

Influences of many cultures have played a part in forming our thoughts about food. Foods need not be heavy and hard to prepare. The Chinese stir-fry technique is very light and quick. Many French people do their shopping daily to have the freshest items possible. It is not uncommon for them to change a recipe because of availability of an item.

The food processor has also helped bring about this change in attitude. Accepting the fact that a machine can chop, blend and grind as well if not better than most cooks, makes it permissible to use an appliance to save time. As consumers, we should judge food by taste and appearance, not by the time it took to prepare.

Be sure to read through the Basics for 30-Minute Meals section, pages 4-13, of this book before you begin to plan a meal. You will find tips on how to make cooking 30-minute meals fun and almost effortless. Less frustration for the cook is what it's all about! The food you choose to prepare should fit into your schedule, not the other way around.

# Breakfast & Brunch Ideas

| | |
|---|---|
| Orange Eye-Opener Drink | Citrus Frappé |
| Apple-Bran Muffins | Oven-Baked French Toast |
| Sweet Butter | "Homemade" Apricot Preserves |
| | |
| Shrimp-Creole Omelet | Crab Brunch Scramble |
| Pineapple-Filled Orange Shells | Fresh-Fruit Salad |
| Raisin-Oatmeal Scones | Orange-Marmalade Coffeecake |

# Lunch Ideas

| | |
|---|---|
| Tuna Delight | Avocado & Beef Croissants |
| Cucumbers in Rice Vinegar | Tomato-Feta Salad |
| Iced Tea | Dry White Wine |
| | |
| Poolside Sandwiches | Far-Eastern Crab Salad |
| Potato Chips | Parmesan Pumpernickel |
| Lemonade Rosé | Dry White Wine |
| | |
| Barbecued Flank-Steak Sandwiches | Cold Guacamole Soup |
| Skillet-Baked Beans | Quesadilla |
| Beer | Margarita-Wine Punch |
| Chocolate-Mint-Frosted Brownies | |

# Dinner Ideas

Halibut en Brochette
Cold Broccoli Salad
Peach-Macaroon Melba

Shrimp-Spaghetti Italiano
Sweet & Sour Spinach Salad
Apricot Tart

Ginger-Glazed Pears & Ham
Caesar Salad
Hot French Bread with Sweet Butter
Scalloped Mashed Potatoes

Orange-Mint Lamb Chops
Spinach-Topped Artichoke Hearts
Fresh-Fruit Salad

Green-Bean Bisque
Dijon Chicken
Tomato-Cheese Vinaigrette
Polka-Dot Rice
Quick Pots de Crème

Mandarin Cornish Hens
Zucchini Vichy
Rice Pilaf

Green-Chili Stroganoff
Egg Noodles
Fluted Carrot Coins

Onion Soup au Gratin
Veal Piccata
Avocado & Mushroom Vinaigrette
Caramel-Pecan Tart

Crab Brunch Scramble, page 83; Fresh-Fruit Salad, page 73; and Orange-Marmalade Coffeecake, page 122.

# Breakfasts & Brunches

Breakfast in today's busy world is built around a fast pace. But that doesn't mean breakfast should be less of a good thing. Fast-to-fix breakfasts can be satisfying. The way to satisfy morning appetites is to serve a variety of taste-tempting meals. Breakfast doesn't have to consist of the classic bacon and eggs. Many an old standby can be updated by adding an element of surprise. Shrimp-Creole Omelet is a basic omelet with shrimp and Creole-style ingredients added. Use this variety of easy yet tasty recipes to create a new breakfast favorite or to plan your next brunch.

One idea for a really quick breakfast is Orange Eye-Opener Drink. It is nutritious as well as fast to make. Serve a homemade condiment, such as Date-Orange Honey, over warm homemade or store-bought flaky croissants.

Mix and match recipes to make your own favorite combinations. Blueberry-Nut Sauce is excellent over pancakes or crepes. Mimosa Fruit Cup could be served as the beginning or finale to breakfast, lunch or dinner.

The leisurely weekend brunch seems to have originated in upper-class British society in the early 1900s. It took about 30 years for it to catch on in the United States. Today, it seems to be the perfect opportunity to entertain or to prepare a more elaborate breakfast showcasing innovative and elegant foods that are fast to fix.

Many brunch or breakfast dishes can be prepared quickly. Then they are popped in the oven or refrigerator, giving you extra time to visit with your guests. For easy serving, prepare pitchers of juice, coffee, tea or cocoa before guests arrive. Then set them out to serve buffet-style.

Brunches range from formal affairs with soufflé and champagne to informal occasions with Oven-Baked French Toast. Some brunches have themes such as a holiday or special occasion. Whatever brunch style you select, take time to plan. Make it a special affair. With a little pre-planning and preparation, there can be ample time to prepare the meal, spend time with guests and add your personal touch to the occasion. 🌺

# Nectarine-Cartwheel Pancakes

*Use this tasty topping for thick Belgian waffles.*

Sour-Cream Topping, see below
2 cups buttermilk baking mix
2 eggs

2 tablespoons butter or margarine, melted
1 pint milk (2 cups)
6 nectarines, sliced

*Sour-Cream Topping:*
1 pint dairy sour cream (2 cups)
1/2 cup packed brown sugar

1/2 teaspoon ground cinnamon

Prepare Sour-Cream Topping; set aside. Grease and preheat a griddle or large skillet. In a medium bowl, combine baking mix, eggs, butter or margarine and milk. Pour batter in 1/2 cup portions onto hot griddle or skillet. When bubbles appear on top of pancakes, turn over. Both sides should be golden brown. When pancakes are done, top each with about 1/3 cup Sour-Cream Topping. Place 4 nectarine slices, cartwheel fashion, in center of each pancake. Makes 4 to 6 servings.

Sour-Cream Topping:
In a small bowl, combine sour cream, brown sugar and cinnamon.

# Cornmeal-Honey Waffles

*Cook these waffles right at the table.*

2 eggs, separated
1 pint milk (2 cups)
1/3 cup butter or margarine, melted
1 cup all-purpose flour
3/4 cup yellow cornmeal
2 teaspoons baking powder

1-1/2 teaspoons baking soda
1/2 teaspoon salt
3 tablespoons honey
2 tablespoons whole-bran cereal,
  if desired

Preheat waffle iron. In a large bowl, beat egg whites until stiff peaks form; set aside. In a medium bowl, combine egg yolks, milk and butter or margarine. Stir in flour, cornmeal, baking powder, baking soda, salt, honey and bran, if desired. When mixture is smooth, fold in beaten egg whites. Pour about 1/3 cup batter onto center of hot waffle iron. Close waffle iron. Bake until steaming stops, about 4 minutes. Remove waffle carefully. Repeat with remaining batter. Makes approximately 6 (8-inch) waffles.

# Mimosa Fruit Cup

*A simple but elegant fruit cup—great to serve for brunch.*

4 medium oranges, chilled
1 cup cold champagne

Fresh mint leaves

Peel oranges, removing as much white pith as possible. Cut oranges into wedges. Place orange wedges in 4 compote dishes. Top each with 1/4 cup cold champagne. Garnish with mint leaves. Makes 4 servings.

# Oven-Baked French Toast

*This French toast is ready all at once, so the cook doesn't have to eat last anymore.*

**15**

| | |
|---|---|
| 4 eggs | 1/2 teaspoon ground nutmeg |
| 1 cup milk | 1 tablespoon sugar |
| 1/2 teaspoon vanilla extract | 8 white-bread slices |

Preheat oven to 500F (260C). Grease a large baking sheet. In a pie plate or other flat dish, beat together eggs, milk, vanilla, nutmeg and sugar. Dip bread slices in egg mixture, coating both sides. Place on greased baking sheet. Bake 10 minutes or until browned and slightly firm. Makes 4 servings.

# French Toast with Apple Slices

*Use whole-wheat, raisin, egg or white bread for this dish.*

**18**

| | |
|---|---|
| 4 eggs | 2 large apples, peeled |
| 1-1/2 cups milk | 3 tablespoons butter or margarine |
| 1/2 teaspoon ground cinnamon | 1/2 cup honey |
| 8 bread slices | 2 teaspoons lemon peel |

Grease and preheat a griddle or large skillet. In a medium bowl, blend eggs, milk and cinnamon. Dip bread slices into egg mixture, 1 at a time; then place on hot griddle or skillet. Cook until golden brown on under side; then turn and cook other side. Cut apples in 1/2-inch slices. Melt butter or margarine in a large skillet. Add apples; sauté until transparent. Add honey and lemon peel. Serve over French toast. Makes 4 to 6 servings.

# Blueberry Waffles

*If you like traditional blueberry pancakes, you'll love these.*

**24**

| | |
|---|---|
| Blueberry-Nut Sauce, opposite | 2 teaspoons baking powder |
| 2 eggs | 1-1/2 teaspoons baking soda |
| 2 cups buttermilk | 1/2 teaspoon salt |
| 2 cups all-purpose flour | 1/3 cup vegetable shortening, melted |

Prepare Blueberry-Nut Sauce; keep warm while preparing waffles. Preheat waffle iron. In a medium bowl, beat eggs. Add buttermilk, flour, baking powder, baking soda, salt and shortening; beat until smooth. Pour about 1/3 cup batter onto center of hot waffle iron. Close waffle iron. Bake until steaming stops, about 4 minutes. Remove waffle carefully. Repeat with remaining batter. Serve each waffle topped with about 1/4 cup Blueberry-Nut Sauce. Makes 6 to 8 servings, about 4 (9-inch-square) waffles or 8 round (7-inch) waffles.

*Use about 1/3 cup batter in a round 7-inch waffle iron or about 2/3 cup batter in a 9-inch-square waffle iron.*

# Blueberry-Nut Sauce

*Great with pancakes or waffles.*

1/2 cup sugar
1/4 teaspoon ground cinnamon
1/8 teaspoon ground nutmeg
2 teaspoons cornstarch

1/2 cup water
1 tablespoon fresh lemon juice
1 cup blueberries
1/2 cup chopped pecans, walnuts or almonds

In a 2-quart saucepan, combine sugar, cinnamon, nutmeg and cornstarch; stir in water and lemon juice. Bring to a boil; reduce heat. Stir in blueberries and nuts. Simmer 5 minutes. Makes 1-3/4 cups.

# "Homemade" Apricot Preserves

*If apricot is not your favorite flavor, try apple butter.*

1 (8-oz.) jar apricot preserves
1/2 cup raisins

1/4 cup chopped pecans

In a small bowl, combine all ingredients; blend well. Preserves have a homemade appearance and flavor. Makes 1-3/4 cups.

# Breakfast Raspberry Sauce

*Serve over pancakes, waffles, crepes or ice cream.*

1 (10-oz.) pkg. frozen raspberries, thawed
1/4 cup sugar
1 tablespoon cornstarch

1/2 cup water
1 tablespoon butter or margarine

Drain raspberries, reserving juice; set berries aside. In a small saucepan, combine raspberry juice, sugar, cornstarch and water. Bring to a boil; cook, stirring constantly, until thickened. Remove from heat. Stir in butter or margarine and reserved berries. Serve hot. Makes 1-2/3 cups.

# Pear-Orange Waffle Topping

*Serve over waffles, pancakes or as a crepe filling.*

1 (29-oz.) can pears
2/3 cup orange marmalade

1 tablespoon fresh lemon juice

Drain pears, reserving 1/3 cup juice. In a small saucepan, combine reserved pear juice, marmalade and lemon juice. Bring to a boil over medium heat, stirring constantly. Thinly slice pears; gently stir into hot sauce. Heat through. Makes 3-1/2 cups.

# How to Make Flower Mangos

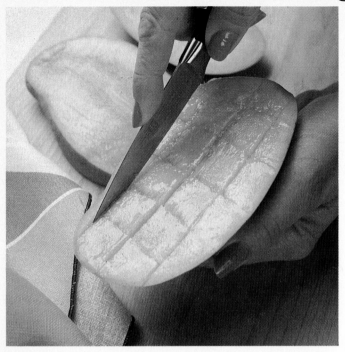 

1/Slice down flat side of mango, removing a slice from each side of the seed. Score flesh by cutting down to but not through the skin of each slice.

2/Turn mango inside-out by pushing skin upward, pushing cut flesh up to fan out. Serve with lime wedges to squeeze over mango.

# Flower Mangos

*Mangos have a large flat seed right down the center.*

**1 ripe mango**
**1 lime**

Cut mango in half by slicing down along the flat side slightly off center; repeat on other side. Remove seed. Score flesh, cutting down to but not through the skin of each half, cutting it into 1/2-inch squares. Turn mango inside-out by pushing skin upward, pushing cut flesh up. It will fan out. Cut lime into quarters. Serve with lime wedges to squeeze over mango. Makes 2 servings.

# Date-Orange Honey

*Serve this flavorful honey on Square Biscuits, page 123, for breakfast.*

**1-1/2 cups honey**          **2 teaspoons grated orange peel**
**1/4 cup orange juice**      **1/2 cup chopped dates**

Combine ingredients in a small saucepan. Cook over medium heat until hot. Serve on waffles, pancakes or French toast. Makes 2-1/4 cups.

# Sunrise Cereal

*The dried-fruit mix can be stored in a tightly covered jar for weeks.*

1/2 cup packed brown sugar
1/4 teaspoon ground cinnamon
1/2 cup diced dates
1/2 cup diced dried apricots
1/2 cup diced dried apples

1/4 cup unsalted, hulled sunflower seeds
4 cups hot cooked cereal, such as
   oatmeal or Cream of Wheat
Cream or milk

In a medium bowl, toss together brown sugar, cinnamon, dates, apricots, apples and sunflower seeds. Fill each of 4 bowls with 1/2 cup cooked cereal. Sprinkle 1 tablespoon dried-fruit mixture over cereal. Top with remaining cooked cereal. Sprinkle 2 tablespoons dried-fruit mixture over each bowl of cereal. Serve with cream or milk. Fruit mix makes 2-1/2 cups or enough for 10 to 12 servings.

# Breakfast in a Roll

*Use quick Brown & Serve rolls for a breakfast surprise.*

6 bacon slices
2 cups shredded sharp Cheddar cheese
   (8 oz.)
1/4 cup mayonnaise

2 tablespoons chopped green onion
2 tablespoons chopped black olives
8 unbaked Brown & Serve rolls

Preheat oven to 400F (205C). In a medium skillet, fry bacon until crisp. Drain bacon; then crumble. In a medium bowl, combine cheese, mayonnaise, green onion, olives and crumbled bacon. Pull rolls apart; remove a small amount of bread from inside each roll half. Stuff rolls with cheese mixture. Put halves back together. Place rolls on a baking sheet. Bake 10 minutes or until cheese is melted. Makes 4 to 8 servings.

# Pita-Pocket Breakfast

*Pita bread is a round, flat bread found in almost all supermarkets.*

1 (3-oz.) pkg. cream cheese,
   room temperature
6 eggs
1/4 cup milk
1/2 teaspoon dried leaf marjoram
1/2 teaspoon salt

1/8 teaspoon pepper
1 teaspoon prepared mustard
3 tablespoons butter or margarine
1 (6-oz.) can sliced black olives, drained
3 pita-bread rounds, cut in half crosswise

Cut cream cheese into 1/2-inch cubes. In a medium bowl, combine cream cheese, eggs, milk, marjoram, salt, pepper and mustard; blend well. In a medium skillet, melt butter or margarine over medium heat. Pour in egg mixture; stir until eggs are set. Stir in olives. Spoon mixture evenly into pita-bread halves. Makes 6 sandwiches.

# Sweet-Sausage Frittata

*Serve this anytime you need a quick fresh meal.*

1/4 cup finely chopped onion
8 oz. sweet Italian sausage, casings removed
1 small zucchini, thinly sliced
1 cup sliced fresh mushrooms
4 eggs
1/2 cup milk

1/2 teaspoon salt
1/8 teaspoon pepper
1/8 teaspoon dried leaf basil
1/8 teaspoon dried leaf oregano
1/4 cup grated Parmesan cheese (3/4 oz.)

In a 9-inch skillet, place onion and sausage. Cook over medium heat, stirring to break sausage into small pieces; drain well. Add zucchini and mushrooms; cook, stirring occasionally, until zucchini is tender. In a medium bowl, beat together eggs, milk, salt, pepper, basil and oregano; pour over sausage mixture. Cook over low heat, lifting edges to allow uncooked portion of egg mixture to run underneath. When eggs are set, sprinkle with cheese. Lift from pan onto a round platter or plate; cut into 4 wedges. Makes 4 servings.

# Perfect Poached Eggs

*Poached-egg rings will give a perfect round egg when cooked, but are not necessary.*

2 qts. water
1/4 cup white vinegar

4 eggs

In a 10-inch skillet, bring water and vinegar to a boil. Reduce heat to a simmer. Gently break eggs into water, 1 at a time. Simmer 3 to 5 minutes, depending on desired doneness of yolk. Gently lift eggs out of water with a skimmer or slotted spoon. Drain well. If eggs are to be used at a later time, place them in cold water. To reheat, place eggs in simmering water 1 to 2 minutes. Makes 4 servings.

# Eggs Florentine

*Serve these individual Florentines for a special brunch or breakfast occasion.*

6 Perfect Poached Eggs, above
2 (10-oz.) pkgs. frozen chopped spinach
1/4 cup butter or margarine
1/4 cup all-purpose flour

1/2 teaspoon salt
1/8 teaspoon red (cayenne) pepper
1 pint milk (2 cups)
1/2 cup shredded Colby cheese (2 oz.)

Prepare Perfect Poached Eggs; keep warm in simmering water. Preheat broiler. Cook spinach according to package directions; drain well. Divide spinach between 6 ramekins or custard cups. Using a spoon, make a depression in center of spinach; place a poached egg in each dish. In a medium saucepan, melt butter or margarine. Stir in flour, salt and red pepper. Add milk; stir until smooth and thickened. Blend in cheese. Pour sauce over eggs and spinach. Broil until top is lightly browned. Makes 6 servings.

# Basic Omelet

*Fill your omelet with shredded cheese and a few chopped fresh herbs.*

| | |
|---|---|
| 6 eggs | 1/8 teaspoon pepper |
| 1/2 cup milk | 2 tablespoons butter or margarine |
| 1/4 teaspoon salt | |

In a medium bowl, beat together eggs, milk, salt and pepper. In a 10-inch skillet, melt butter or margarine over medium-high heat. When butter or margarine begins to bubble, pour in egg mixture. After 2 to 3 minutes, when eggs begin to set on the bottom, gently lift up outer edges with a spatula, letting uncooked egg mixture flow underneath. When eggs are completely set, slide out onto a warm platter. Fill half with desired filling; fold other half over top. Makes 2 to 3 servings.

# Shrimp-Creole Omelet

*Shrimp make any meal seem extra special.*

| | |
|---|---|
| 2 tablespoons butter or margarine | 1 (15-oz.) can tomato sauce |
| 1/2 cup chopped onion | 5 oz. cooked baby shrimp (1 cup) |
| 1/4 cup chopped green bell pepper | 1/4 cup sliced pimiento-stuffed green olives |
| 1 garlic clove, crushed | 1 Basic Omelet, above |

In a medium saucepan, melt butter or margarine. Add onion, green pepper and garlic; sauté over medium heat. Add tomato sauce, shrimp and olives. Simmer 5 minutes. Prepare Basic Omelet. Spoon shrimp mixture into omelet, reserving 1/2 cup to spoon over top. Makes 4 servings.

# Pineapple-Mushroom Omelet

*A complete breakfast in one omelet, including fruit.*

| | |
|---|---|
| 5 bacon slices | 1/4 cup diced pineapple |
| 1 (8-oz.) pkg. frozen hash-brown potatoes, thawed | 4 eggs, beaten |
| | 1/2 cup milk |
| 1 cup sliced fresh mushrooms | 1/4 cup sliced green onions |

In a large skillet, fry bacon until crisp; remove bacon, reserving drippings. Drain bacon; then crumble. Sauté potatoes in bacon drippings until tender. Add mushrooms and pineapple; flatten mixture into bottom of skillet. In a medium bowl, combine eggs and milk; pour over potato mixture. Cover and cook over medium-low heat until set. Top with crumbled bacon and green onions. To serve, cut in wedges. Makes 4 servings.

# How to Make Granola Baked Apples

1/Scoop out inside of each apple, leaving a 1/2-inch-thick shell.

2/Top each baked apple with sour cream or yogurt. Garnish with a mint sprig, if desired.

**30**

## Granola Baked Apples

*Try this for dessert, too.*

**4 cooking apples**
**3/4 cup granola cereal**
**2 tablespoons brown sugar**

**Water**
**1/2 cup dairy sour cream or yogurt**

Preheat oven to 400F (205C). Cut a 1/2-inch slice from top of each apple; remove and discard core. Scoop out and reserve apple pulp, leaving a 1/2-inch shell. Chop apple pulp. In a medium bowl, combine chopped apple pulp, cereal and brown sugar. Fill scooped-out apples, mounding tops. Place in a shallow baking dish; pour water to a depth of 1/4 inch in dish. Cover with foil. Bake 25 minutes or until apples are tender. Serve with sour cream or yogurt. Makes 4 servings.

## Tip

*If pie filling or sugar syrup spills into a hot oven, sprinkle spilled juice immediately with salt. Then allow to burn crisp. Clean-up will then be easy.*

# Lunches & Light Meals

Lunch is one of the meals I enjoy creating most. There are no hard and fast rules that pertain to lunch. It can be a wine and cheese picnic, a bite on the run, or even a formal sit-down luncheon with guests. Many of the lunch recipes will also make great midnight meals, such as Individual Spinach Soufflés.

Lunch is a good meal to serve foods that you purchase ready prepared—not just the deli foods that first come to mind, but some of the ready-prepared foods we take for granted, like cheese.

Sausage Kabobs are great to prepare before guests arrive. Then, if you are heading out for a bike ride or other activity, the kabobs will be ready and waiting to cook quickly when you arrive home hungry.

Sandwiches are always a favorite for lunch. Poolside Sandwiches are good travelers. Make them ahead, pack them in a cooler and take them to the pool or beach. They are really satisfying for hungry appetites.

Grilled Chili-Cheese Sandwiches are a delicious take-off on the standard grilled-cheese sandwiches. Include chilies and tomato slices with two types of cheese for this tasty treat. It's sure to please the after-the-game crowd.

For a light early afternoon luncheon, serve Cheese Soufflé along with a tasty quick bread and fruit salad. What could be easier and more delightful? This soufflé is delicious whether served for breakfast, lunch or dinner.

When it's cold outside and you want a hearty hot soup for lunch, try Sicilian Meatball Soup. Small meatballs cook quickly in the hot beef broth. Young children will especially like this soup with the thin egg noodles.

Although often thought to be from Mexico, Chimichangas are actually from southern Arizona. Meat, beans and typical Mexican seasonings are enclosed in a thin flour tortilla. Deep-fried until golden brown, they are generally served with salsa and sour cream. They are excellent for lunch or a late-evening snack. 🌺

# Baked Broccoli Frittata

*A* frittata *is an omelet with the filling blended into the eggs.*

2 tablespoons butter or margarine
2 cups chopped fresh broccoli or
   1 (10-oz.) pkg. frozen chopped broccoli,
   slightly thawed
1 cup thinly sliced onions
1 cup sliced fresh mushrooms
1 cup fresh or frozen whole-kernel corn
8 eggs

1 cup milk
3/4 cup shredded Monterey Jack cheese
   (3 oz.)
1/2 teaspoon salt
1/8 teaspoon pepper
1 tablespoon chopped fresh basil or
   1/2 teaspoon dried leaf basil,
   crumbled

Preheat oven to 350F (175C). In a large ovenproof skillet, melt butter or margarine. Add broccoli, onions, mushrooms and corn; sauté until broccoli is tender. In a medium bowl, lightly beat eggs. Blend in milk, cheese, salt, pepper and basil. Pour egg mixture into skillet with sautéed vegetables. Place skillet in oven; bake 15 to 20 minutes or until eggs are set. Makes 6 servings.

# Tortilla Frittata

*Curry and yogurt give this dish a slight East Indian flair.*

1 lb. lean pork sausage
1 large onion, chopped
1/2 cup sliced fresh mushrooms
1 cup chopped tomatoes
1 teaspoon curry powder
1 garlic clove, minced

6 eggs
1/4 cup milk
Vegetable oil
6 (8-inch) flour tortillas
1 cup plain yogurt or
   dairy sour cream (8 oz.)

In a large skillet, sauté sausage and onion until sausage is no longer pink; stir frequently to crumble sausage. Add mushrooms, tomatoes, curry powder and garlic; sauté 3 minutes. In a small bowl, beat eggs and milk. Lightly oil a 10-inch skillet or large griddle. Place 1 tortilla in skillet or on griddle; spread with about 3/4 cup sausage mixture. When tortilla starts to sizzle, pour 1/3 cup egg mixture over sausage. Cook until egg mixture has set. Top with yogurt. Repeat with remaining tortillas, sausage mixture, egg mixture and yogurt. Makes 6 servings.

# Green-Chili Strata

*Most stratas have to set overnight. Prepare and bake this one all at one time.*

6 white-bread slices
1/4 cup butter or margarine
1 small onion, chopped
2-1/2 cups milk
4 eggs, beaten

1 (4-oz.) can diced green chilies
2 cups shredded Cheddar cheese (8 oz.)
1 teaspoon salt
3 drops hot-pepper sauce

Preheat oven to 375F (190C). Grease an 8-inch-square baking pan; set aside. Cut bread into 1-inch cubes. In a small skillet, melt butter or margarine. Add onion; sauté over medium heat until transparent. In a large bowl, combine milk, eggs, chilies, cheese, salt and hot-pepper sauce. Add sautéed onion and bread cubes to milk mixture; stir to blend. Pour mixture into greased pan. Bake 20 to 25 minutes or until center is firm. Makes 6 servings.

**20**

# Individual Spinach Soufflés

*Serve as a side dish or as the main entree for a light meal.*

| | |
|---|---|
| **2 tablespoons butter or margarine** | **3 eggs, separated** |
| **2 tablespoons all-purpose flour** | **1 (10-oz.) pkg. frozen chopped spinach,** |
| **1 cup milk** | **thawed, drained** |
| **1/2 teaspoon salt** | **1/2 teaspoon cream of tartar** |
| **1/2 cup shredded Cheddar cheese (2 oz.)** | **4 (10-inch) flour tortillas** |

Preheat oven to 425F (220C). In a small saucepan, melt butter or margarine; stir in flour until smooth. Cook 1 minute. Add milk, stirring constantly. Simmer mixture, stirring constantly until slightly thickened, about 2 minutes. Remove from heat. Stir in salt and cheese until cheese melts. In a small bowl, beat egg yolks; stir in 1/4 cup hot milk mixture. Then pour egg-yolk mixture into milk mixture in saucepan; blend well. Stir in spinach. In a small bowl, beat egg whites and cream of tartar until stiff. Fold spinach mixture into beaten egg whites. Wet each tortilla by holding it under running water. Cut each tortilla in half. Fit 2 tortilla halves into each of 4 individual soufflé dishes, forming a shell that rises above the dish about 2 inches. Divide spinach mixture evenly between dishes. Bake 10 minutes. Reduce heat to 375F (190C). Bake 10 minutes longer. Makes 4 servings.

**30**

# Cheese Soufflé

*Cheese soufflés are so versatile they can be served for breakfast, lunch or dinner.*

| | |
|---|---|
| **2 tablespoons butter or margarine** | **1 teaspoon Worcestershire sauce** |
| **2 tablespoons all-purpose flour** | **2 cups shredded sharp Cheddar cheese** |
| **1 cup milk** | **(8 oz.)** |
| **1 teaspoon salt** | **5 eggs, separated** |
| **1-1/2 teaspoons dry mustard** | **1/4 teaspoon cream of tartar** |

Grease and flour a 2-quart soufflé dish; set aside. Preheat oven to 400F (205C). In a medium saucepan, melt 2 tablespoons butter or margarine over medium heat. Stir in 2 tablespoons flour. Cook 1 minute. Add milk, salt, mustard and Worcestershire sauce. Cook, stirring constantly, until thickened. Stir in cheese until melted. In a medium bowl, beat egg whites and cream of tartar until stiff; set aside. In a large bowl, beat egg yolks until blended. Gradually stir cheese mixture into egg yolks. Fold in egg whites. Pour into prepared soufflé dish. Bake 20 minutes or until center is set. Makes 4 to 6 servings.

**Tip**

*Eggs separate best when cold; egg whites beat best at room temperature.*

# How to Make Onion Tart

1/Line a 10-inch tart pan with pastry dough; trim edges evenly.

2/Pour cheese mixture into tart pan; top with sautéed onions.

**30**

# Onion Tart

*Slicing all these onions with a food processor saves time and tears.*

| | |
|---|---|
| 1 (10-inch) unbaked tart shell | 2 eggs, slightly beaten |
| 1/4 cup butter or margarine | 1/2 teaspoon salt |
| 3 cups thinly sliced onions | 1/8 teaspoon pepper |
| 2 cups cottage cheese (1 lb.) | |

Preheat oven to 425F (220C). Bake tart shell 5 to 7 minutes. Meanwhile, in a large skillet, melt butter or margarine. Add onions; sauté until transparent. In a medium bowl, combine cottage cheese, eggs, salt and pepper; pour into baked tart shell. Reduce heat to 375F (190C). Top with sautéed onions. Bake 20 minutes. Makes 6 to 8 servings.

# Tuna Delight

*Try this for a light supper some time.*

Cheddar-Cheese Sauce, see below
3 English muffins, split
1 (6-1/2-oz.) can water-pack tuna, drained

1/4 cup mayonnaise
1 (8-oz.) can crushed pineapple, drained
1/4 cup fresh bean sprouts

*Cheddar-Cheese Sauce:*
2 tablespoons butter or margarine
2 tablespoons all-purpose flour
1 cup milk
1/4 teaspoon salt

1 teaspoon Dijon-style mustard
1/2 cup shredded sharp Cheddar cheese
   (2 oz.)

Prepare Cheddar-Cheese Sauce; keep warm. Toast English muffins. In a medium saucepan, combine tuna, mayonnaise, pineapple and bean sprouts. Cook over medium heat until warm through. Spoon hot tuna mixture on toasted English-muffin halves. Ladle Cheddar-Cheese Sauce over top. Makes 6 servings.

**Cheddar-Cheese Sauce:**
In a small saucepan, melt butter or margarine, Stir in flour; cook over medium heat 1 minute. Add milk, a little at a time, stirring until smooth. Bring mixture to a simmer; cook until slightly thickened. Stir in salt, mustard and cheese. Cook until sauce starts to boil.

# Avocado & Beef Croissants

*Good croissants make any filling taste better.*

4 croissants
1 large avocado, peeled
1/2 cup mayonnaise
2 tablespoons fresh lemon juice
1 teaspoon dried leaf tarragon, crumbled

2 green onions, chopped
4 lettuce leaves
8 oz. roast beef, thinly sliced
1 tomato, thinly sliced
1/2 cup alfalfa sprouts

Arrange croissants on a baking sheet; place in a cold oven. Turn oven to 400F (205C); heat 10 minutes. Meanwhile, in a medium bowl mash avocado. Stir in mayonnaise, lemon juice, tarragon and green onions. Remove warm croissants from oven; split each lengthwise. On bottom of each croissant, place a lettuce leaf, some roast beef and a tomato slice. Spread each with avocado mixture; top each with alfalfa sprouts. Replace top of each croissant. Makes 4 sandwiches.

# Gazpacho Relish

*Serve this relish as a topping for hamburgers.*

1 large tomato, peeled, chopped
1/2 large cucumber, peeled, chopped
2 tablespoons chopped green bell pepper
1 tablespoon thinly sliced green onion

1 tablespoon cider vinegar
1/4 teaspoon sugar
1/4 teaspoon salt

In a small bowl, combine all ingredients. Cover and refrigerate. Makes 1-1/4 cups.

# How to Make Chinese Tortilla Roll-Ups

1/Cut chicken into narrow strips.

2/Spread warm tortillas with Hoisin Sauce.

## Chinese Tortilla Roll-Ups

*Hoisin sauce is a unique-flavored sauce available in the Oriental section of most supermarkets.*

| | |
|---|---|
| 8 (10-inch) flour tortillas | 1 cup fresh bean sprouts |
| 2 tablespoons sesame oil or vegetable oil | 1/2 cup chicken broth or stock |
| 3/4 lb. boneless chicken breast | 3 tablespoons soy sauce |
| 1/4 cup sliced green onions | 1 tablespoon dry sherry |
| 1/2 teaspoon minced gingerroot | 2 teaspoons sugar |
| 1 garlic clove, minced | 2 teaspoons cornstarch |
| 1/2 cup sliced fresh mushrooms | 1/2 cup Hoisin sauce |

Preheat oven to 350F (175C). Lay tortillas out flat on oven racks, 2 deep, if necessary. Warm tortillas 5 to 10 minutes. Do not leave them too long because they will become crisp and impossible to roll. Heat oil in a wok or large skillet. Cut chicken into narrow strips; stir-fry in hot oil until cooked. Stir in green onions, gingerroot, garlic, mushrooms and bean sprouts; stir-fry 3 minutes. In a small bowl, combine broth or stock, soy sauce, sherry, sugar and cornstarch; add to wok or skillet. Stir until meat and vegetables are well coated and sauce is thickened. Spread warm tortillas with Hoisin sauce. Spoon about 1/4 cup chicken mixture down the center of a tortilla. Fold bottom end of tortilla up 2 inches; then roll up from 1 side. Repeat with remaining chicken mixture and tortillas. Serve warm. Makes 4 servings.

# Barbecued Flank-Steak Sandwiches

**25**

*A gas barbecue is a great timesaver, but still gives that wonderful barbecued flavor.*

Basting Sauce, see below
1 (1-1/2-lb.) beef flank steak
Salt and pepper
6 long French rolls, split lengthwise

Butter or margarine
12 (1-oz.) slices Muenster cheese
Guacamole, page 45
Salsa, page 45

*Basting Sauce:*
1/4 cup olive oil
2 tablespoons lemon juice

1 teaspoon Worcestershire sauce

Preheat broiler or barbecue grill. Prepare Basting Sauce. Brush both sides of beef with Basting Sauce. Season lightly with salt and pepper. Cook beef, 4 inches from heat, 6 minutes on each side for medium-rare. Cook longer for desired doneness. Baste beef again before turning. Place cooked beef on a cutting board; cut in thin 1/4-inch diagonal slices. To assemble sandwiches, butter both cut sides of rolls. Top each bottom roll half with 2 cheese slices. Place beef slices on cheese. Top with Guacamole and Salsa. Place other roll half on top. Makes 6 hearty sandwiches.

**Basting Sauce:**
In a small bowl, combine all ingredients; blend well.

# Sausage Kabobs

**17**

*A tasty and attractive sandwich.*

4 smoked knackwurst or other sausage
12 (1-1/2-inch) squares fresh pineapple
12 (1-1/2-inch) squares green bell pepper
Quick Sweet & Sour Sauce, page 101

4 long French rolls, split lengthwise
Butter
4 (1-oz.) slices Muenster cheese

Preheat broiler. Cut each sausage crosswise into 3 equal pieces. On each of 4 skewers, alternate 3 sausage pieces, 3 pineapple squares and 3 green-pepper squares. Arrange filled skewers on a broiler pan. Broil, 6 inches from heat, 8 to 10 minutes, turning frequently. Baste often with Quick Sweet & Sour Sauce. Butter rolls; broil briefly to warm through. Place a cheese slice on bottom half of each warm roll; then slide a kabob onto cheese. Top with remaining roll half. Makes 4 servings.

# Creamy Mustard-Horseradish Sauce

**5**

*Great to serve with a corned-beef sandwich.*

1 cup dairy sour cream
2 teaspoons prepared mustard

1 heaping tablespoon prepared horseradish

In a small bowl, combine all ingredients. Add more horseradish for a hotter flavor. Makes 1 cup.

# Grilled Chili-Cheese Sandwiches

*Grilled-cheese sandwiches with a surprise filling.*

| | |
|---|---|
| 1/4 cup butter or margarine,<br>    room temperature | 2 large canned chilies |
| 4 sourdough-bread slices | 2 large tomato slices |
| 2 Monterey-Jack-cheese slices | 2 tablespoons dairy sour cream |
| | 2 Cheddar-cheese slices |

Preheat griddle or large skillet. Spread butter or margarine on 1 side of each bread slice. Place 2 bread slices, buttered-side down, on hot griddle or skillet. Top each slice with Monterey Jack cheese, chili, tomato, sour cream and Cheddar cheese. Top each with remaining bread, buttered-side up. After 2 to 3 minutes when bread is golden brown, turn sandwiches to toast other side. Bread should be golden brown on each side. Makes 2 sandwiches.

# Poolside Sandwiches

*Wrap sandwiches tightly in plastic wrap; then take them along with you.*

| | |
|---|---|
| 4 long French rolls, split lengthwise | 4 ham slices |
| Mayonnaise | 4 Monterey Jack cheese slices |
| Dijon-style mustard | 1 red onion, thinly sliced |
| 4 lettuce leaves | 4 dill pickles, thinly sliced |

Spread roll halves with mayonnaise. Spread bottom roll halves with mustard. Top each roll with lettuce, ham, cheese, onion and dill pickle. Top each with remaining roll halves. Wrap tightly in plastic wrap or foil to retain freshness. Refrigerate until ready to serve. Makes 4 servings.

# Spinach Lasagna

*Purchase a good brand of marinara sauce to save preparation time.*

| | |
|---|---|
| 4 oz. lasagna noodles | 1/4 cup chopped green onions |
| 1 cup cottage cheese (8 oz.) | 1 teaspoon dried leaf oregano |
| 1/2 cup dairy sour cream | 1/2 teaspoon salt |
| 4 eggs | 1-1/2 cups marinara sauce (12 oz.) |
| 2 (10-oz.) pkgs. frozen chopped spinach,<br>    thawed, drained | 1 lb. Monterey Jack cheese, thinly sliced |
| | 1/2 cup grated Parmesan cheese (1-1/2 oz.) |

Preheat oven to 375F (190C). Cook noodles according to package directions; drain well. In a medium bowl, beat together cottage cheese, sour cream, eggs, spinach, green onions, oregano and salt. In an 11" x 7" baking pan, layer 1/2 the noodles, cottage-cheese mixture, marinara sauce, Monterey Jack cheese and Parmesan cheese. Repeat with remaining ingredients. Bake 20 minutes. Makes 6 to 8 servings.

# How to Make Chimichangas

1/Fold in 4 sides of each tortilla, envelope-style. Secure with a wooden pick.

2/Fry stuffed tortillas until golden brown on both sides. Drain on paper towels.

**18**

# Chimichangas

*Freeze leftovers for another quick meal.*

1 lb. ground beef
8 oz. chorizo sausage, casings removed
1 medium onion, chopped
1/4 cup chopped fresh cilantro
1 (4-oz.) can diced green chilies

1 cup shredded Cheddar cheese (4 oz.)
12 (10-inch) flour tortillas
Vegetable oil
Salsa, page 45
Dairy sour cream

In a large skillet, fry ground beef, chorizo and onion until meats are cooked; stir frequently to break up meat and blend well. Drain off excess fat. Stir in cilantro, chilies and cheese. Place about 1/3 cup meat mixture near center of a tortilla. Fold in 4 sides, envelope-style; secure with a wooden pick. Repeat with remaining tortillas and meat filling. Pour oil to a 3/4-inch depth in a large skillet. Heat oil to 370F (190C) or until a 1-inch cube of bread turns golden brown in 50 seconds. Fry 3 or 4 stuffed tortillas at a time until both sides are golden brown; drain on paper towels. Cover lightly with foil or place in a warm oven to keep warm. Serve with Salsa and sour cream for topping. Makes 12 Chimichangas or 6 servings.

## Tip

*To reheat frozen Chimichangas, place in a single layer on a baking sheet. Bake at 350F (175C) for 25 minutes.*

# Appetizers

Appetizers set the pace for a meal. They create a first impression that should say "Great things are to follow." Color, imagination and uniqueness come into play. Most importantly, appetizers must taste great.

Appetizers are really a first course. They can be served casually in the living room or more formally at the table. Use appetizers to whet the appetite, not discourage it. Don't overdo it when planning appetizers. The trend is toward lighter meals. Spiced nuts and a glass of wine are great openers, and easy to fix.

Fresh vegetables are the perfect appetizer as crudités for dips and spreads. To save time but retain attractiveness, buy vegetables that need minimal preparation. Cherry tomatoes need only be washed. Zucchini and cucumbers can be cut in round slices or sticks without peeling. Red or green bell peppers slice quickly and are colorful. For a special touch, quickly cut green-onion fans. Place them in ice water until ready to arrange vegetables. Cut slices of *jícama*, a root vegetable similar to a potato. Using a flower-, star- or heart-shape cookie cutter, cut out three or four interesting shapes to give a more formal appearance to your vegetables. For an attractive serving container, line a basket or platter with a lush layer of parsley. It holds its shape and appearance well over a long period of time. Then arrange vegetable pieces on parsley. Leftover vegetables can be wrapped in plastic and refrigerated. They will be a ready and welcome addition to a salad anytime in the next few days.

Quick-to-fix appetizers, such as Chili-Cheese Chips and Camembert Fondue, can keep you from being frazzled when hungry people are awaiting their meal. Pop these into the oven and out comes a tasty and interesting appetizer. Baking frees you to do other things while the oven does your work. Have a selection of appetizers, such as Tuna Antipasto and Sherry-Sesame Sticks, that you can put together from items stored in your pantry. That way, you can have something ready when you need it in a hurry.

When selecting an appetizer as part of a 30-minute meal, consider ingredients and their preparation requirements. Then decide in what order to prepare the recipes. If some foods need to marinate in a dressing or there is an herb combination that could benefit from chilling a few minutes, prepare that recipe first. Chilling or warming, as the recipe directs, gives maximum flavor to each dish.

Garnishing appetizers is important. Edible garnishes are preferable and they look fresh and natural. Fresh basil or dill sprigs tucked in, if that is the herb used in the recipe, gives a clue as to flavor as well as a fresh appearance. Freshly grated cheese, chopped nuts or chopped parsley all add color and flavor.

Use these ideas to combine appetizers with your meals or to make a meal from appetizers.

---

## Bacon-Wrapped Artichoke Hearts    *Photo on page 46.*

*Use extra-lean bacon to minimize shrinkage and spattering.*

**6 bacon slices**
**12 peeled, cooked baby shrimp**

**1 (6-oz.) jar marinated artichoke hearts,**
**drained, cut in quarters**

Preheat broiler. Cut each bacon slice in half crosswise. Place 1 shrimp and 1 artichoke-heart piece together; wrap with a bacon piece. Secure with a wooden pick. Arrange on a broiler pan. Broil, 4 inches from heat, 5 to 7 minutes or until bacon is cooked. Makes 12 appetizers.

**Variation**
Substitute oysters for shrimp.

## Sausage Roll-Ups

*Serve with soup or salad, or as an appetizer.*

**1 (8-oz.) tube refrigerator crescent-roll dough**
**Dijon-style mustard**

**1 (5-1/2-oz.) pkg. mini smoked-sausage**
**links, precooked**

Preheat oven to 375F (190C). Unroll crescent rolls; cut each in half lengthwise. Spread dough halves with mustard. Place a sausage at the wide end of 1 dough piece; roll up securely. Repeat with remaining dough and sausages. Arrange on a baking sheet. Bake 15 minutes or until golden brown. Makes 16 servings.

## Chili-Cheese Chips

*Use any firm cheese, such as Swiss, Cheddar or Monterey Jack.*

**4 oz. chili-flavored cheese**

Preheat oven to 350F (175C). Lightly grease a baking sheet. Do not use non-stick aerosol. Cut cheese into 1/2-inch squares, about 1/4 inch thick. Place cheese squares, 2 inches apart, on greased baking sheet. Bake 3 to 5 minutes or until melted flat. Remove from oven; cool until set. Peel off cheese chips. Makes about 30.

# Salmon Appetizer

*Canned salmon on your pantry shelf can quickly solve the appetizer question.*

1 (7-3/4-oz.) can salmon, drained, boned
1/2 cup sliced celery
1/4 cup chopped green onions
1/4 cup mayonnaise

1/4 cup chili sauce
1 tablespoon fresh lemon juice
2 teaspoons prepared horseradish
Curly leaf lettuce

In a medium bowl, toss together salmon, celery and green onions. Cover and refrigerate until ready to serve. In a small bowl, combine mayonnaise, chili sauce, lemon juice and horseradish. Refrigerate until ready to serve. To serve, line 4 cocktail glasses with lettuce leaves. Spoon salmon mixture evenly into lettuce-lined glasses. Spoon mayonnaise mixture over each serving. Makes 4 servings.

# Italian Salmon Canapés

*This is a quick antipasto.*

1 (16-oz.) can cannellini beans, drained
1 (7-3/4-oz.) can salmon, drained, boned
1/2 cup chopped tomato
1/2 cup chopped onion

1/3 cup Italian salad dressing
Salt and pepper
Small pieces of melba toast

In a medium bowl, combine beans, salmon, tomato, onion and salad dressing. Season to taste with salt and pepper. Serve with small pieces of toast. Makes 3 cups.

# Anchovy Canapés

*Room-temperature cream cheese makes spreading easy and prevents tearing the bread.*

16 party-size rye-bread slices
1 (3-oz.) pkg. cream cheese,
    room temperature
Sliced cherry tomatoes

1 (2-oz.) can anchovies,
    cut into 1/2-inch pieces
Watercress sprigs

Spread bread slices with cream cheese. Top each with 3 tomato slices and an anchovy piece. Garnish with watercress sprigs. Makes 16 canapés.

**Variation**

Substitute kippered herring for anchovies, if desired.

# Tuna Antipasto

*Easy to prepare ahead as you can refrigerate this two to three days.*

3/4 cup olive oil
6 tablespoons fresh lemon juice
1 tablespoon sugar
1 teaspoon salt
1 teaspoon dried leaf tarragon
2 (6-1/2-oz.) cans water-pack tuna, drained

1/2 cup pimiento-stuffed green olives
8 oz. whole small mushrooms, cut in half
8 oz. peeled, cooked shrimp
3 tomatoes, cut in wedges
4 green onions, sliced

In a small bowl, combine oil, lemon juice, sugar, salt and tarragon; blend well. In a medium bowl, combine tuna, olives, mushrooms, shrimp, tomatoes and green onions. Pour oil mixture over tuna mixture; toss to coat well. Cover and refrigerate at least 15 minutes before serving. Drain, reserving marinade. Arrange tuna, olives, mushrooms, shrimp, tomatoes and green onions on a large platter. Serve with marinade. Makes 6 servings.

# Oysters Rockefeller

*Serve with small plates and spoons.*

1 (10-oz.) pkg. frozen creamed spinach
12 large oysters with open shells
Hot-pepper sauce

3 tablespoons butter or margarine
1/4 cup grated Parmesan cheese (3/4 oz.)
1/4 cup dry breadcrumbs

Cook spinach according to package directions. Preheat broiler. Place 1 oyster in each shell; discard remaining shells. Put 1 drop hot-pepper sauce on each oyster. Melt butter or margarine in a small saucepan; stir in cheese and breadcrumbs. Top each shell with cooked spinach; sprinkle cheese mixture over spinach. Place filled shells on a broiler pan; broil, 4 inches from heat, until heated through and crumbs begin to brown. Makes 4 to 6 servings.

# Chafing-Dish Mushrooms

*Serve this easy appetizer as a side dish, also.*

1 lb. fresh mushrooms
2 tablespoons butter or margarine

1 pint dairy sour cream (2 cups)
1 (1-oz.) pkg. buttermilk-dressing mix

Clean and trim mushrooms. Melt butter or margarine in a large skillet. Add mushrooms; sauté until slightly cooked. Stir in sour cream and dressing mix. Heat through but do not boil. Transfer to a chafing dish set in a hot-water bath. Keep warm over a candle. Makes 8 appetizer servings.

 **Tip**

*Sour cream will curdle if boiled. Fresh cream will not curdle if simmered gently.*

# How to Make Stuffed Baby Gouda

1/Cut a thin slice off top of cheese; scoop out inside, leaving a 1/4-inch-thick shell.

2/Garnish by circling with parsley; top with a black-olive slice. Serve with crackers.

**10**

## Stuffed Baby Gouda

*The red-wax outer shell makes an attractive container for this spread.*

1 (8-oz.) Gouda cheese
1 (3-1/2-oz.) can sliced black olives, drained
1/4 cup dry white wine

1 tablespoon chopped green onion
Parsley
Assorted wheat crackers

Cut off a thin slice from the top of cheese; scoop out inside, leaving a 1/4-inch shell. Place scooped-out cheese in a blender or food processor. Add black olives, wine and green onion. Process until blended but not smooth. Spoon mixture into shell, mounding the top. Refrigerate until ready to serve. May be made up to 3 days ahead. Garnish by circling base of cheese with parsley; top with a black-olive slice. Serve with assorted wheat crackers. Makes 4 to 6 servings.

**10**

## Quick Brie Spread     *Photo on pages 78 and 79.*

*Heat and eat.*

8 oz. Brie cheese
2 apples, cored

Preheat oven to 350F (175C). Place cheese in an ovenproof dish. Bake 5 minutes or until melted. Cut apples into 1/4-inch wedges. Serve melted cheese with apple wedges. Makes 4 servings.

# Tasty Braunschweiger Spread

*A quick recipe to prepare using a food processor.*

8 oz. braunschweiger or liver sausage
1 (8-oz.) pkg. cream cheese,
   room temperature

1/2 cup chutney, finely chopped
Assorted crackers or breads

In a medium bowl or food processor, combine braunschweiger or liver sausage, cream cheese and chutney; blend well. Place in a serving dish. Refrigerate 15 minutes or longer before serving. Serve with crackers or breads. Makes 2-1/2 cups.

**Variation**

Substitute 1 envelope dry-onion-soup mix for chutney.

# Curry-Cheese Spread

*Refrigerate this spread up to four days.*

1 cup shredded Cheddar cheese (4 oz.)
1 (8-oz.) pkg. cream cheese,
   room temperature
1/4 cup dry white wine

3/4 teaspoon curry powder
1/3 cup chopped walnuts
1/3 cup raisins
Apple and pear wedges

In a medium bowl or food processor, combine Cheddar cheese, cream cheese, wine and curry powder. Process until smooth. Stir in walnuts and raisins. Serve spread with fruit wedges. Makes 3 cups.

# Beer-Cheese Fondue

*If you don't have a food processor to shred cheese, save time and buy shredded cheese.*

1 garlic clove, cut in half
1 (12-oz.) can flat beer
4 cups shredded Cheddar cheese (1 lb.)
4 cups shredded Monterey Jack cheese (1 lb.)
2 tablespoons cornstarch

2 teaspoons chili powder
1 (4-oz.) can diced green chilies
1 sourdough-bread loaf, cut in 1-inch cubes
Fresh-vegetable pieces

Rub a ceramic fondue pot or medium saucepan with garlic halves. Add beer; heat slowly until beer begins to simmer. In a large bowl, combine cheeses, cornstarch and chili powder. Gradually stir cheese mixture into warm beer until melted and smooth. Stir in chilies. Keep warm over a candle. If using a saucepan, transfer mixture to a fondue pot and keep warm. Serve fondue with bread cubes and fresh vegetables. Makes 8 servings.

# Camembert Fondue

*Removing the cheese rind results in a milder flavor.*

8 oz. Camembert cheese, rind removed
1-1/2 cups cottage cheese (12 oz.)

1/4 cup dairy sour cream
Breadsticks

Cut Camembert cheese into 1-inch cubes. Place in a small saucepan with cottage cheese. Cook, stirring constantly, over medium-low heat until cheeses melt. Stir in sour cream. Serve with breadsticks for dipping. Makes 2-3/4 cups.

# Creamy Blue-Cheese Dip

*Use leftovers as a dressing for green salad.*

1 (3-oz.) pkg. cream cheese, room temperature
2 oz. blue cheese, room temperature
1 cup dairy sour cream
1 (2-1/2-oz.) jar dried beef, minced

1/4 teaspoon garlic salt or
  1/8 teaspoon garlic powder
1/2 teaspoon Worcestershire sauce
Assorted raw-vegetable pieces

In a medium bowl, combine cream cheese and blue cheese. Stir in sour cream, beef, garlic salt or garlic powder, and Worcestershire sauce. Serve with vegetables. Makes 2-1/2 cups.

# Super Bean Dip

*Everyone seems to have a variation of this favorite dip.*

2 (16-oz.) cans refried beans
1 (8-oz.) pkg. cream cheese
1 cup dairy sour cream
1 (1.25-oz.) pkg. taco-seasoning mix

1 teaspoon hot-pepper sauce
1 cup shredded Monterey Jack cheese (4 oz.)
Tortilla chips

In a large saucepan, combine beans, cream cheese, sour cream, taco-seasoning mix and hot-pepper sauce. Cook over medium heat until blended and hot. Pour into a serving dish. Top with shredded cheese. Serve with tortilla chips. Makes 6 cups.

# Quesadilla

*This is so good, you can easily make a meal out of it.*

1 (10-inch) flour tortilla
1/2 cup shredded Cheddar cheese (2 oz.)
2 tablespoons canned diced green chilies
1 green onion, chopped

Salsa, below
1/2 cup dairy sour cream
1/2 cup Guacamole, below

Preheat a griddle or large skillet. Place tortilla on hot griddle or skillet. Cover half the tortilla with cheese, chilies, green onion and 3 tablespoons Salsa. Fold plain tortilla half over top; press down gently. Using a spatula, turn tortilla over to heat other side. Serve warm, topped with sour cream and Guacamole. Spoon additional Salsa over top, if desired. Makes 1 Quesadilla or 2 to 3 appetizer servings.

# Salsa    *Photo on page 34.*

*A tasty sauce, great for chip dipping or as a topping for Quesadilla, above.*

1 (16-oz.) can tomatoes
1 (4-oz.) can diced green chilies
1 tablespoon chopped fresh cilantro

3 green onions, finely chopped
1 garlic clove, minced
Salt and pepper

In a blender or food processor, finely chop tomatoes. In a medium bowl, combine chopped tomatoes and juice, chilies, cilantro, green onions and garlic. Season to taste with salt and pepper. Cover and refrigerate until ready to serve. Makes 2-1/2 cups.

# Guacamole

*Originally popular as a dip, guacamole adds flavor to eggs, salads or sandwiches.*

2 avocados
2 tablespoons fresh lemon juice
1 tomato, finely chopped
1 (4-oz.) can diced green chilies

1/2 cucumber, finely chopped, if desired
Hot-pepper sauce
Salt and pepper

In a medium bowl or food processor, puree avocados with lemon juice. Blend in tomato, chilies and cucumber, if desired. Add hot-pepper sauce to taste, 1 drop at a time. Season to taste with salt and pepper. Makes 2-1/2 cups.

# Irish-Style Nachos

*Potato slices are used in place of traditional tortilla chips.*

2 medium potatoes, unpeeled
2 tablespoons vegetable oil
1/2 cup shredded Cheddar cheese (2 oz.)

1/4 cup chopped fresh cilantro
1/2 cup dairy sour cream
1/2 cup Salsa, page 45

Preheat broiler. Slice potatoes 1/8 inch thick. Heat oil in a large skillet. Add potato slices; sauté until tender. Place sautéed potatoes on an ovenproof platter. Sprinkle cheese over potato slices. Broil until cheese melts. Top with cilantro, sour cream and Salsa. Makes 4 servings.

# Crabmeat Nachos

*The ultimate in nachos!*

1 (10-oz.) pkg. tortilla chips
6 oz. Dungeness crabmeat
2 cups grated Cheddar cheese (8 oz.)

3/4 cup Salsa, page 45
1/4 cup chopped green onions

Preheat broiler. Spread tortilla chips in a single layer on an ovenproof platter. Break crabmeat into small pieces; sprinkle over chips. Sprinkle cheese over crabmeat. Broil 3 minutes or until cheese melts. Immediately before serving, top with Salsa and green onions. Makes 6 servings.

# Sherry-Sesame Sticks

*Serve these with your favorite cream soup.*

1 cup all-purpose flour
1/4 cup vegetable shortening
1 cup shredded sharp Cheddar cheese (4 oz.)

1/4 cup dry sherry
2 tablespoons sesame seeds

Preheat oven to 450F (230C). In a medium bowl, combine flour, shortening and cheese until crumbly. Blend in sherry to form a pastry-like dough. Gather dough in a ball; place on a baking sheet. Roll out dough to a 9-inch square. Sprinkle sesame seeds over dough; gently press seeds into dough with a rolling pin. Cut dough into 3'' x 1'' rectangles. Bake 8 to 10 minutes or until crisp. Cool on wire racks. Store in an airtight container. Makes 27 sticks.

Left to right: Blue-Cheese-Stuffed Pecans, page 48; Chili-Almond Bites, page 48; Sherry-Sesame Sticks, above; and Bacon-Wrapped Artichoke Hearts, page 39.

**15**

# Curried Peanuts

*A quick and tasty treat that can be prepared on very short notice.*

1 cup dry-roasted peanuts
1 tablespoon butter or margarine, melted

1/2 teaspoon curry powder
1/8 teaspoon garlic powder

Preheat oven to 350F (175C). In a medium bowl, combine peanuts, butter or margarine, curry powder and garlic powder. Stir well to coat peanuts. Spread peanuts evenly on a baking sheet. Bake 10 minutes. Cool slightly to allow peanuts to regain their crunchiness. Makes 1 cup.

**10**

# Chili-Almond Bites     Photo on page 46.

*Almonds regain their crunchiness as they cool.*

2 tablespoons butter or margarine
3/4 teaspoon chili powder
1/2 teaspoon seasoned salt

1-1/2 cups whole unblanched almonds (8 oz.)
1/2 teaspoon salt

In an 8-inch skillet, melt butter or margarine; stir in chili powder and seasoned salt. Add almonds; sauté 3 minutes, stirring to coat almonds with seasoning. Spread almonds on paper towels. Sprinkle salt over almonds; cool. Serve almonds warm or at room temperature. Makes 1-1/2 cups.

**12**

# Blue-Cheese-Stuffed Pecans     Photo on page 46.

*When pressed for time, put cheese mixture out and let guests spread their own.*

2 tablespoons Danish or other blue cheese,
  room temperature
2 tablespoons cream cheese,
  room temperature

8 oz. large pecan halves (1-3/4 cups)

In a small bowl, whip together blue cheese and cream cheese until fluffy. Spread mixture on flat surface of 1 pecan half. Top with another pecan half, sandwich style. Repeat with remaining pecans and cheese spread. Makes 1/4 cup spread.

**10**

# Candied Orange Pecans

*Keep these nuts in an airtight jar for a quick dessert.*

1 cup sugar
1/2 cup water
Grated peel of 1 orange

1/4 teaspoon vanilla extract
2 cups pecan halves

In a medium saucepan, bring sugar, water and orange peel to a boil. Boil 5 minutes. Remove from heat; stir in vanilla. Stir in pecans until all are well coated. Spread coated pecans on waxed paper to cool. Makes 2 cups.

# How to Make Stuffed Jalapeño Peppers

1/Cut each pepper in half; remove seeds. Place pepper halves in a bowl of ice water.

2/Prepare salmon filling; carefully spoon into pepper halves.

**12**

## Stuffed Jalapeño Peppers

*Be sure to remove all seeds from peppers because they are the hottest part.*

1 (12-oz.) can whole small jalapeño peppers
1 (7-3/4-oz.) can salmon, drained, boned
1 hard-cooked egg, finely chopped

1/4 cup dairy sour cream
1/4 teaspoon garlic salt

Cut each pepper in half; remove seeds. Place pepper halves in a bowl of ice water. In a medium bowl, combine salmon, egg, sour cream and garlic salt. Pat peppers dry with paper towels. Stuff pepper halves with salmon mixture. Arrange on a platter. Makes 4 to 6 servings.

**30**

## Cream-Cheese-Stuffed Mushrooms

*Sure to be the first to disappear at your next party.*

8 oz. fresh mushrooms
1 (3-oz.) pkg. cream cheese,
   room temperature

2 tablespoons grated Parmesan cheese
1/8 teaspoon garlic salt

Preheat oven to 350F (175C). Clean and trim mushrooms; remove stems. In a small bowl, combine cream cheese, Parmesan cheese and garlic salt until smooth. Spoon mixture into each mushroom, slightly rounding tops. Place stuffed mushrooms in an ovenproof dish. Bake 20 minutes or until warm. Makes 6 servings.

# Soups

When you think of soup, do you visualize a stock pot simmering on the stove for hours? Great-tasting soup can be made easily in minutes. Whether velvety smooth or chunky and hearty, soup preparation does not have to take long. Save time by using your blender or food processor for chopping and pureeing.

Soups are divided into two types: clear and cream. Clear soup usually has meat and vegetable pieces added. Cream soup has a cream base with pureed vegetables or meat added. For either, the base is often a meat stock. Don't hesitate to use a good canned stock or broth, bouillon granules or bouillon cubes in place of homemade stock. With the addition of fresh, tasty ingredients, your guests will think it simmered all day. For cream soups, use cream, half and half, sour cream, yogurt or milk. Do not boil a cream soup after the milk product has been added. It will curdle or separate if boiled.

Soup comes under several different titles, but all mean soup.

**Broth**—Clear, thin soup made by boiling meat or vegetables in water.

**Bouillon**—Concentrated clear broth.

**Consommé**—Clear soup made by boiling meat and sometimes vegetables in water. Strain the soup and serve hot or as a cold jelly.

**Cream Soup**—Broth that has been thickened, usually with flour or cornstarch, using cream or milk with vegetables, fish or chicken.

**Chowder**—A thick fish, meat or vegetable soup, usually flavored with salt pork and prepared with milk or cream.

**Bisque**—Usually a shellfish soup with a cream-sauce base.

**Fruit Soup**—Generally made with fresh, frozen, dried or canned fruits. Serve chilled or warm.

Soups can be very creative because most of the ingredients are readily interchangeable. If you plan to make Green-Bean Bisque, but have broccoli on hand, substitute broccoli for beans in equal amounts and you have a new soup!

Most cream soups taste good served hot or cold. Zucchini-Dill Cream Soup is a good example. Cold soup may be new to some, but it's very refreshing. It's a nice touch either to chill or warm the soup bowls ahead of time. This helps retain the correct serving temperature.

A large tureen of soup is very inviting, but also think of serving soups in mugs, compote dishes or even small casseroles. Complete your soup with an attractive garnish. Use an herb sprig, a dollop of sour cream, a few gratings of cheese or nutmeg, or even a fresh-strawberry or lemon slice, if serving a fruit soup.

Here are a few suggestions that make cooking soups quicker and easier:

● Cut vegetables into small, even-size pieces for fast cooking.

● Clear soup can be converted to a cream soup by adding cream, yogurt, milk or sour cream.

● Soups are a good way to use leftovers. Leftovers are generally precooked, so soup preparation time will be less.

● Keep in mind the relative cooking time of ingredients. Add dense, long-cooking items first. Then add those items that require less cooking.

● If you are adding uncooked pasta or rice, be sure to add extra liquid. Pasta and rice absorb liquid as they cook.

● Be selective with seasonings. Taste before adding salt, pepper or extra herbs.

● If soup is too spicy, simmer 3 to 4 medium-potato pieces in it; then discard potato pieces.

● Cooking time for soups with large pieces of meat or vegetables may be shortened by using a pressure cooker.

---

**28**

# Chicken Gumbo

*Filé powder is made from dried young sassafras leaves.*

| | |
|---|---|
| 2 tablespoons butter | 2 cups diced cooked chicken or turkey |
| 1/2 cup chopped onion | 1/2 teaspoon salt |
| 1/4 cup chopped green bell pepper | 1/2 teaspoon dried leaf basil |
| 1/2 cup sliced fresh mushrooms | 1/4 teaspoon dried leaf thyme |
| 1 garlic clove, crushed | 1/8 teaspoon pepper |
| 1 qt. chicken broth or stock (4 cups) | 1 tablespoon cornstarch |
| 3/4 cup uncooked long-grain white rice | 1/4 cup cold water |
| 2 cups fresh or frozen sliced okra | 1 teaspoon filé powder, if desired |
|    (about 8 oz.) | Hot cooked rice |

In a large saucepan, melt butter over medium heat. Add onion, green pepper, mushrooms and garlic; sauté lightly. Stir in broth or stock, uncooked rice, okra, chicken or turkey, salt, basil, thyme and pepper. Bring to a boil. Reduce heat and simmer 15 minutes or until rice is tender. In a small bowl, combine cornstarch and 1/4 cup water; stir into soup. Cook, stirring constantly, 5 minutes or until slightly thickened. Remove from heat; stir in filé powder, if desired. Serve over cooked rice. Makes 6 servings.

---

# Tip

*Add filé powder after removing gumbo from heat. If cooked too long, filé powder becomes stringy.*

**20**

# New Year's Eve Oyster Stew

*Eating oyster stew on New Year's Eve is said to bring luck for the whole year.*

2 (10-oz.) jars Pacific oysters
2 tablespoons butter or margarine
1 medium onion, diced
1/4 cup thinly sliced celery
2 tablespoons cornstarch

1 pint chicken broth or stock (2 cups)
1 pint whipping cream (2 cups)
Salt and pepper
Oyster crackers

In a large saucepan, cook oysters in their liquid over medium heat until edges begin to curl. Remove from saucepan; set aside. In same saucepan, melt butter or margarine. Add onion and celery; sauté until onion is transparent. Stir in cornstarch; cook 1 minute. Gradually stir in broth or stock and whipping cream. When soup begins to simmer, stir in cooked oysters with their liquid. Season to taste with salt and pepper. Serve with oyster crackers. Makes 6 servings.

**25**

# Savory Seafood Soup

*Chopping these vegetables in a food processor saves time.*

2 tablespoons olive oil
1 medium onion, finely chopped
1 green bell pepper, seeded, chopped
2 garlic cloves, crushed
2 (6-oz.) cans tomato paste
2 (8-oz.) bottles clam juice
3 cups chicken broth or stock
1/2 cup dry red wine

1 bay leaf
1 teaspoon dried leaf basil, crumbled
1 tablespoon chopped fresh cilantro
3 drops hot-pepper sauce
12 clams in shells
8 oz. medium uncooked shrimp,
  peeled, deveined
1-1/2 lbs. seabass, cut in 1-inch cubes

In a 6-quart saucepan, heat oil. Add onion, green pepper and garlic; sauté until onion is transparent. Stir in tomato paste, clam juice, broth or stock, wine, bay leaf, basil and cilantro. Cover and simmer 5 minutes. Add hot-pepper sauce, clams, shrimp and seabass. Cover and simmer 5 to 10 minutes or until clams open, shrimp are pink and seabass is cooked. Remove and discard bay leaf and any clams that do not open. Makes 6 to 8 servings.

 **Tip** ──────────────────────────────────────

*Hot-pepper sauce should always be added at the end of the cooking time because it loses its hot taste as it cooks.*

# Tuna-Dill Chowder

*Canned salmon is a colorful substitute for tuna.*

1/4 cup butter or margarine
1/4 cup all-purpose flour
1 qt. milk (4 cups)
1 (6-1/2-oz.) can water-pack tuna, drained

1 (10-oz.) pkg. frozen chopped broccoli
1/2 teaspoon dill weed
1 tablespoon fresh lemon juice

In a large saucepan, melt butter or margarine over medium heat. Stir in flour. Cook 1 minute. Gradually add milk, stirring until mixture begins to thicken. Add tuna, broccoli, dill weed and lemon juice. Simmer 10 minutes. Makes 4 to 6 servings.

### Variation
**Tuna-Noodle Soup:** Add 1 cup water and 1 cup thin egg noodles at the same time tuna is added. Simmer 15 minutes or until noodles are tender.

# Creamed Crab & Spinach Soup

*Crab adds an elegant touch to basic cream soup.*

1 (6- to 8-oz.) pkg. frozen crabmeat, thawed
1 (10-oz.) pkg. frozen chopped spinach
3 tablespoons butter or margarine
1/2 cup chopped onion
2 tablespoons all-purpose flour

1/2 teaspoon salt
1/8 teaspoon ground nutmeg
1 pint chicken broth or stock (2 cups)
1 pint half and half (2 cups)

Defrost and drain frozen crabmeat. Cut crabmeat into 1/2-inch pieces, set aside. Cook spinach according to package directions; drain well. In a large saucepan, melt butter or margarine. Add onion; sauté until tender. Blend in flour, salt and nutmeg. Add broth or stock, stirring constantly. Bring to a boil. Reduce heat. Stir in half and half, crabmeat pieces and spinach. Heat through; do not boil. Makes 4 to 6 servings.

# Spicy Sausage Soup

*Each guest can add his own condiments.*

1 lb. hot Italian sausage, casings removed
1 cup thinly sliced carrots
1/3 lb. green beans, cut in
   1-1/2-inch lengths (about 1 cup)
2 medium onions, thinly sliced
5 cups beef broth or stock

2 medium tomatoes, cut in 1/2-inch wedges
1 (16-oz.) can baby corn cobs, drained
Salt and pepper
Condiments: dairy sour cream,
   shredded Cheddar cheese, lime wedges,
   sliced black olives and Salsa, page 45

Crumble sausage in a 5-quart saucepan; add carrots, green beans and onions. Sauté over medium heat 5 minutes or until sausage is no longer pink; drain off fat. Add broth or stock, tomatoes and corn. Cover and simmer 10 minutes. Season to taste with salt and pepper. Ladle into soup bowls. Serve with a choice of condiments. Makes 6 to 8 servings.

**25**

# Hearty Potato-Ham Chowder

*An especially appealing soup for a cold evening.*

2 tablespoons butter or margarine
2 medium potatoes, peeled, diced
1/2 cup chopped green bell pepper
1/4 cup sliced green onions
2-1/3 cups water
1 teaspoon salt
1/4 teaspoon paprika

1/8 teaspoon pepper
3 tablespoons all-purpose flour
1 pint milk (2 cups)
1 (10-oz.) pkg. frozen whole-kernel corn
1 cup diced cooked ham
Chopped parsley

In a large saucepan, melt butter or margarine. Add potatoes, green pepper and green onions; cook until slightly tender. Add 2 cups water, salt, paprika and pepper. Cover and simmer until potatoes are tender. In a small bowl, combine flour and 1/3 cup water; stir into potato mixture. Gradually stir in milk; cook until slightly thickened. Stir in corn and ham; heat through. Sprinkle parsley over top. Makes 6 servings.

**15**

# Ham & Sweet-Potato Soup

*Serve this hearty soup with Pineapple-Filled Orange Shells, page 72.*

2 tablespoons vegetable oil
1/2 cup sliced celery
1/2 cup thinly sliced green onions
1 qt. beef broth or stock (4 cups)
1 tablespoon prepared mustard

1 tablespoon brown sugar
1/4 teaspoon ground allspice
1-1/2 cups (1-inch) cooked-ham cubes
1 (16-oz.) can sweet potatoes, drained,
    cut in round 1/4-inch-thick slices

In a large saucepan, heat oil. Add celery and green onions; sauté until onions are transparent. Stir in broth or stock, mustard, brown sugar and allspice. Add ham and sweet potatoes. Cover and simmer 5 minutes or until warm through. Makes 5 to 6 servings.

## Tip

*For a thicker soup, combine 1/4 cup all-purpose flour and 1/2 cup water. Stir flour mixture into soup before adding ham. Cook 2 to 3 minutes, stirring frequently, until slightly thickened. Proceed as directed.*

# How to Make Fresh-Vegetable Cream Soup

1/Puree cooked vegetables and other ingredients until smooth or to desired texture.

2/Serve Vegetable Cream Soup garnished with fresh herbs.

**12**

## *Fresh-Vegetable Cream Soup*

*Use your imagination and whatever fresh vegetables you have on hand.*

| | |
|---|---|
| **1-1/2 lbs. fresh vegetables or<br>  2 (10-oz.) pkgs. frozen vegetables,<br>  thawed**<br>**1 cup chicken broth or stock**<br>**1/8 teaspoon pepper** | **1 tablespoon chopped fresh herbs or<br>  1 teaspoon dried leaf herbs,<br>  such as dill, basil or oregano**<br>**1 pint whipping cream (2 cups)**<br>**Salt** |

Clean and trim fresh vegetables. Steam or cook vegetables in the microwave until crisp-tender. In a blender or food processor, combine hot vegetables, broth or stock, pepper and herbs; puree until smooth or leave slightly chunky, if desired. Pour into a medium saucepan. Stir in whipping cream. Season to taste with salt. Heat to desired serving temperature. Makes 4 to 6 servings.

# Cream of Corn Soup

*Omit the chicken broth and make a great vegetable side dish.*

2 (10-oz.) pkgs. frozen whole-kernel corn
1-1/2 cups chicken broth or stock
1 cup dairy sour cream
1 cup whipping cream

1/3 cup grated Parmesan cheese (1 oz.)
1 tablespoon sugar
1/2 teaspoon salt

In a large saucepan, combine corn and broth or stock. Cover and bring to a boil. Reduce heat and simmer 5 minutes. Stir in sour cream, whipping cream, cheese, sugar and salt. Heat to desired serving temperature; do not boil. Makes 4 to 6 servings.

# Zucchini-Dill Cream Soup

*Garnish with a fresh dill sprig for a really fresh look.*

1 lb. fresh zucchini, trimmed,
    cut in 1-inch lengths
1 cup dairy sour cream

4-1/2 teaspoons fresh dill or
    1-1/2 teaspoons dill weed
1 cup chicken broth or stock

Steam zucchini or cook in the microwave until tender. In a food processor or blender, puree cooked zucchini with sour cream and dill. Pour pureed mixture into a medium saucepan; stir in broth or stock. For a thinner soup, add more broth or stock. Reheat or refrigerate, depending on desired serving temperature; do not boil. Makes 4 servings.

# Mashed-Potato Soup

*Instant potatoes form the base for this soup.*

1 pint milk (2 cups)
1-3/4 cups chicken broth or stock
2 cups instant mashed-potato flakes

3 tablespoons sliced green onion
1/2 cup buttermilk salad dressing

In a medium saucepan, bring milk and broth or stock to a simmer. Stir in potato flakes, green onion and salad dressing. Cover and simmer 5 minutes. Serve warm or refrigerate and serve cold. Makes 4 servings.

# How to Make Carrot Flowers

1/Cut 5 evenly spaced V-shape strips of carrot, 1/8 inch deep, lengthwise down the carrot.

2/Cut carrot into 1/8-inch-thick slices. Slices will resemble flowers.

**8**

## Oriental Mushroom Soup

*Photo on page 59.*

*A good way to use small leftovers of beef, pork or chicken.*

1 qt. chicken broth or stock (4 cups)
1/2 cup thinly sliced carrots or
   Carrot Flowers, above
1/2 cup thinly sliced fresh mushrooms

3/4 cup julienned strips of cooked beef,
   pork or chicken
Cilantro sprigs

In a large saucepan, bring broth or stock and carrots to a boil. Reduce heat; add mushrooms and meat strips. Heat until desired serving temperature. Ladle into soup bowls; garnish with cilantro. Makes 4 servings.

**15**

## Chinese Vegetable Soup

*Ground ginger gives a special flavor.*

1 lb. ground beef
1-1/2 qts. beef broth or stock (6 cups)
1/4 cup ketchup
2 tablespoons soy sauce
1/2 teaspoon ground ginger

1/2 teaspoon salt
5 to 6 green onions, diagonally cut in
   1-inch pieces (1/2 cup)
1/4 cup dry sherry
1/2 cup thinly sliced radishes

In a large saucepan, brown ground beef over medium heat; drain well. Stir in broth or stock, ketchup, soy sauce, ginger, salt, green onions and sherry. Bring to a boil; reduce heat. Simmer 5 minutes. Pour into a tureen. Garnish with radishes. Makes 6 to 8 servings.

# Tomato-Rice Bisque

**20**

*For best flavor, use high-quality tomato juice.*

1/4 cup butter or margarine
1/4 cup all-purpose flour
3 cups milk
1 cup tomato juice
1 tablespoon chopped fresh basil or
   1 teaspoon dried leaf basil

1 teaspoon Worcestershire sauce
1 cup tomatoes, seeded, finely chopped
1/2 cup quick-cooking rice
Fresh basil leaves

In a 2-quart saucepan, melt butter or margarine. Stir in flour until blended. Gradually stir in milk, tomato juice, basil and Worcestershire sauce. Cover and bring to a boil. Reduce heat. Add tomatoes and rice. Cover and simmer 10 minutes, stirring occasionally. Serve hot, garnished with fresh basil leaves. Makes 5 to 6 servings.

# Green-Bean Bisque

**22**

*Serve cold or hot, depending on the temperature outside.*

1 lb. fresh green beans or
   1 (10-oz.) pkg. frozen green beans,
   thawed
2 tablespoons butter or margarine

1 medium onion, finely chopped
3 cups chicken broth or stock
Dairy sour cream
1/4 cup slivered almonds

Wash and trim fresh beans; cut in 1-inch pieces. In a medium saucepan, melt butter or margarine over medium heat. Add onion and fresh or frozen beans; sauté until onion is transparent. Add broth or stock. Cover and simmer 10 minutes or until beans are tender. Puree mixture in a blender or food processor. Mixture may need to be pureed in 2 or 3 batches. Reheat or refrigerate, depending on desired serving temperature. Garnish each serving with a dollop of sour cream and a few slivered almonds. Makes 4 to 6 servings.

# Onion Soup au Gratin

**28**

*Use your food processor to slice onions quickly and uniformly.*

6 tablespoons butter or margarine
6 medium onions, thinly sliced
1-1/2 qts. strong beef broth or stock
   (6 cups)
1 teaspoon salt

1/4 teaspoon pepper
1 teaspoon dried leaf marjoram, crumbled
6 (1/2-inch-thick) French-bread slices
1-1/2 cups shredded Swiss cheese (6 oz.)
2 tablespoons grated Parmesan cheese

In a large saucepan, melt butter or margarine. Add onions; sauté over medium heat until soft but not browned. Add broth or stock, salt, pepper and marjoram. Bring to a boil. Reduce heat and simmer 15 minutes. Adjust seasonings as desired. Preheat broiler. Ladle soup into 6 ovenproof bowls. Place a French-bread slice on top of each serving. Top each serving with 1/4 cup Swiss cheese and 1 teaspoon Parmesan cheese. Place bowls under broiler, 4 inches from heat, until cheese melts. Serve hot. Makes 6 servings.

Top to bottom: Oriental Mushroom Soup, page 57; Cold Guacamole Soup, page 60; and Tomato-Rice Bisque, above.

**25**

# Cold Guacamole Soup   *Photo on page 59.*

*Ripe avocados give slightly to gentle pressure. Store ripe avocados in the refrigerator.*

4 ripe avocados, peeled, chilled
1 pint chicken broth or stock,
  chilled (2 cups)
1 tablespoon fresh lemon juice
1/2 teaspoon salt

1/4 teaspoon pepper
1/4 teaspoon garlic powder
1 cup dairy sour cream
1 cup half and half
1/4 cup Salsa, page 45

In a blender or food processor, puree avocados with 1 cup broth or stock. In a large bowl or tureen, combine avocado mixture, remaining broth or stock, lemon juice, salt, pepper and garlic powder. Stir in sour cream and half and half until smooth. Refrigerate until ready to serve. Garnish each serving with 1 tablespoon Salsa. Makes 4 servings.

**30**

# Vichyssoise

*Serve this classic potato soup in iced servers.*

2 tablespoons butter or margarine
1/2 cup chopped onion
2 cups peeled, thinly sliced potatoes
  (3/4 lb.)
1 pint chicken broth or stock (2 cups)

1/4 teaspoon salt
1/8 teaspoon white pepper
1 cup whipping cream
Chopped chives, if desired

In a large skillet, melt butter or margarine over medium heat. Add onion and potatoes; sauté until onion is transparent. Add broth or stock, salt and white pepper. Bring to a boil. Cover and simmer over low heat 15 minutes or until potatoes are tender. Pour hot mixture into a blender or food processor; process until smooth. Soup may need to be pureed in 2 or 3 batches. Pour into a medium bowl. Stir whipping cream into soup. Refrigerate until well chilled. Serve chilled soup garnished with chives, if desired. Makes 4 servings.

*Chill soup quickly by adding 2 ice cubes per serving. Stir 30 seconds; discard any remaining ice.*

# Strawberry-Wine Soup

*Enjoy this colorful soup year-round.*

1-1/2 cups fresh or frozen whole,
   unsweetened strawberries
1/4 cup sugar
2 teaspoons cornstarch
1/2 cup dry white wine

1/2 (3-inch) cinnamon stick
3/4 cup whipping cream
Whole strawberries
Mint leaves

Thaw strawberries if frozen. Puree 1-1/2 cups strawberries in a blender or food processor. In a medium saucepan, combine sugar and cornstarch. Gradually blend in wine and strawberry puree. Add cinnamon stick. Bring to a boil, stirring constantly. Boil 2 minutes; cool. Remove cinnamon stick. Stir in whipping cream. Cover and refrigerate. Stir to blend before serving. Garnish each serving with whole strawberries and mint leaves. Makes 4 servings.

# Cherry-Dumpling Soup

*A soft dough makes more tender dumplings.*

1 qt. water (4 cups)
1 qt. frozen or canned pitted red
   tart cherries
2/3 cup sugar

1-1/4 cups all-purpose flour
1/2 teaspoon salt
1-1/2 cups boiling water
1 egg

In a large saucepan, combine 4 cups water, cherries and sugar. Simmer over medium heat 10 minutes or until cherries are warm. In a medium bowl, combine flour and salt. Using a fork, blend in boiling water; then blend in egg. When dough is completely blended, drop by teaspoonfuls into simmering cherry mixture. Cook 10 minutes or until dumplings are completely cooked. Makes 4 to 6 servings.

# Scandinavian Fruit Soup

*Serve leftover soup chilled for breakfast.*

3 cups apple juice
1/2 cup dried apricots
1/4 cup golden raisins
1/3 cup sugar
1 (3-inch) cinnamon stick

2 medium apples, peeled, finely chopped
1 teaspoon grated lemon peel
4-1/2 teaspoons cornstarch
2 tablespoons sliced almonds

In a large saucepan, combine 2-1/2 cups apple juice, apricots, raisins, sugar, cinnamon stick, apples and lemon peel. Bring to a boil over medium heat. Reduce heat and simmer 10 minutes or until apricots are tender. In a small bowl, combine remaining 1/2 cup apple juice and cornstarch; stir into soup. Cook, stirring constantly, 3 to 4 minutes or until soup is slightly thickened. Remove cinnamon stick. Garnish each serving with sliced almonds. Makes 4 to 5 servings.

# Salads

At one time, salads were considered a palate cleanser or a way to get enough greens for a nutritional meal. Today they are often meals in themselves and are made from more than lettuce or other greens. Make a pasta salad with fresh vegetables. Add a few meat slices and you have a tasty, nutritious, colorful and attractive meal; but it's a salad!

Basic greens can be transformed rapidly into a star attraction with the addition of special homemade dressings or a surprise ingredient. Look in the supermarket produce department for items you rarely or never use in a salad. Check your refrigerator for leftovers you could include. Freshly made dressings, creamy or vinegar-oil type, taste fresh and usually need only a minute to make.

For a quick refreshing salad, top fresh-pineapple slices with strawberry yogurt. This could also be used as a snack. Add a little cottage cheese to a vinaigrette-dressed green salad. You've added some protein and created something new from an old standby.

Individual salad plates give the salad definition and keep the dressing from combining with other foods. Place salad plates in the freezer at least ten minutes before they are needed. Chilling salad plates ahead of time keeps salads cold longer at the table.

If you are really pressed for time, serve the salad on a large platter. Show off your salad by lining the plate with something eye-catching, like red cabbage, spinach leaves or thinly sliced cucumber placed in a ring. Use chopped nuts or coconut for accent. Or, serve the salad in the hollowed-out shell of a piece of fruit.

Most salads are served cold, so keep the ingredients chilled until you are ready to use them. Don't leave them out at room temperature. Make the salad early enough to give it time to chill and blend the flavors. Some salads, such as Oriental Chicken Salad, are served warm; others, like Pineapple-Chili Salad, are even served hot.

Red, ripe tomatoes and cool, crisp greens are a tried and true standby. With your addition of a fresh homemade dressing, like Creamy Parmesan Dressing or Pesto Dressing, you're set to serve. Whichever salad you choose, homemade dressing is a must and takes only a few minutes to prepare.

It's best to tear lettuce or other greens into bite-size pieces. Other ingredients can be cut quickly into various shapes and sizes to add visual interest. Try cubes, slices, rounds, wedges and julienne strips, but be sure all are bite size. It is very awkward to cut salads at the table.

Pre-preparation of salad is a good way to save time. Often, greens and vegetables can be prepared the day before. Store in plastic bags to pre-serve freshness. Do not combine different fruits or vegetables in the same bag because flavors will blend and become indistinct. Once washed, the quality of greens and vegetables starts to diminish. Vegetables that discolor, such as potatoes, avocados and mushrooms, should not be prepared ahead.

Salads can play many roles, depending on their ingredients. A salad can be a meal in itself or a delightful side to an entree. Let your creativity run wild in creating salads. Any ingredient should be given consideration. Meat, fruit and vegetables in any combination can prove very tasty.🌼

**12**

# Sweet & Sour Spinach Salad

*Fresh spinach is available year-round, which makes this salad perfect anytime.*

| | |
|---|---|
| 1 bunch spinach | 2 teaspoons prepared mustard |
| 6 bacon slices | 1/4 cup red-wine vinegar |
| 1 onion, chopped or 5 green onions, sliced | 1/4 teaspoon curry powder, if desired |
| 2 tablespoons brown sugar | 3 cups sliced fresh mushrooms |

Clean spinach; tear into bite-size pieces. Place in a salad bowl; cover with a damp paper towel. Refrigerate spinach until ready to serve. In a large skillet, fry bacon until crisp; remove bacon, reserving drippings. Drain bacon; then crumble. Sauté onion in bacon drippings until transparent. Stir in brown sugar, mustard, vinegar and curry powder, if desired. Keep dressing warm until ready to serve. To serve, in a large bowl, toss together spinach, crumbled bacon and mushrooms. Add warm dressing; toss lightly. Serve immediately. Makes 4 servings.

### Variations

Add 1-1/4 ounces crumbled blue cheese, 6 to 8 tomato wedges and 1 thinly sliced avocado to spinach mixture. Omit curry powder from dressing mixture. Proceed as above.

To make a main-dish salad, add 1 cup diced cooked chicken or 4 hard-cooked eggs, cut in wedges, to the spinach mixture. Proceed as above.

# Tip

*For quick chopped hard-cooked eggs, grate eggs.*

# Caesar Salad

*An all-time-favorite salad in many restaurants.*

**1 large head romaine lettuce**
**Caesar Dressing, see below**

**Caesar Dressing:**
**1/2 cup olive oil**
**1/4 cup fresh lemon juice**
**2 to 5 anchovies, if desired**
**1 egg**
**1 garlic clove**

**1 teaspoon Worcestershire sauce**
**1/2 cup grated Parmesan cheese (1-1/2 oz.)**
**1 teaspoon salt**
**1/4 teaspoon pepper**

Tear lettuce into bite-size pieces; place in salad bowl. Cover with a damp paper towel. Refrigerate until ready to serve. Prepare Caesar Dressing. To serve, toss lettuce lightly with Caesar Dressing. Makes 4 to 6 servings.

**Caesar Dressing:**
Combine ingredients in a blender or food processor. Process until well blended. Use immediately or refrigerate until ready to serve.

# Curry-Green-Pea Salad    *Photo on pages 78 and 79.*

*Curry seems to make even simple ingredients exotic.*

**1 (16-oz.) pkg. frozen green peas**
**1 cup fresh or frozen cooked baby shrimp**
**1/3 cup mayonnaise**

**1/4 teaspoon curry powder**
**1/4 cup slivered almonds**

To thaw peas and shrimp, place in a colander. Run cold water over peas and shrimp to thaw slightly; drain well. In a medium serving bowl, combine mayonnaise and curry powder. Add drained peas, shrimp and 3 tablespoons almonds; toss to mix. Garnish with 1 tablespoon almonds. Refrigerate until ready to serve. Makes 6 servings.

# Cold Broccoli Salad

*Why not serve a salad for your vegetable course?*

**2 (10-oz.) pkgs. frozen chopped broccoli**
**1/2 cup sliced water chestnuts**
**1 medium tomato, chopped**

**1 cup mayonnaise**
**1/4 cup soy sauce**

Cook broccoli according to package directions; drain in a colander. Run cold water over cooked broccoli to cool; drain well. In a medium bowl, combine cooked broccoli, water chestnuts and tomato. In a small bowl, blend mayonnaise and soy sauce; pour over broccoli mixture. Toss to coat well. Serve immediately or refrigerate until ready to serve. Makes 6 servings.

# How to Make Oriental Chicken Salad

1/Cook bean or rice threads in hot oil until puffed.

2/Serve salad on a nest of cooled bean or rice threads.

**15**

## Oriental Chicken Salad

*Serve this salad warm or cold.*

Oriental Dressing, see below
Vegetable oil
2 oz. bean or rice threads
3 cups diced cooked chicken (about 1 lb.)
1 cup diagonally sliced celery

1/2 cup drained pineapple chunks
1/4 cup coarsely chopped fresh cilantro
6 green onions, thinly sliced
1/2 cup cashews

*Oriental Dressing:*
1/4 cup rice vinegar
1/2 cup vegetable oil
2 tablespoons soy sauce

2 tablespoons dry sherry
1 tablespoon sugar
1/4 teaspoon ground ginger

Prepare Oriental Dressing; set aside. Pour oil into a large skillet to a 1-inch depth. Heat to 375F (190C) or until a 1-inch cube of bread turns golden brown in 50 seconds. Add half the bean or rice threads. They will immediately puff up. Push threads down into oil to cook completely. Remove threads from oil; drain on paper towels. Repeat with remaining threads. In a large bowl, combine chicken, celery, pineapple, cilantro and green onions. Toss with Oriental Dressing. On a platter, shape a nest of cooled bean or rice threads; mound chicken salad on top. Garnish with cashews. Makes 4 to 6 servings.

**Oriental Dressing:**
Combine all ingredients in a medium bowl; blend well. Refrigerate until ready to serve.

# Chef's Salad

*Check your refrigerator and pantry for possible additions to this catch-all salad.*

4 oz. Swiss cheese
8 oz. cooked ham
8 oz. cooked turkey or chicken
2 medium tomatoes
1 head lettuce
1 (8-oz.) can sliced beets, drained

1 (10-oz.) pkg. frozen or canned
  asparagus spears, drained or
  3/4 lb. fresh asparagus, parboiled
Creamy Parmesan Dressing, page 73;
  Blue-Cheese Dressing, below;
  and Pesto Dressing, below

Cut cheese, ham and turkey or chicken in 3-inch-long narrow strips. Cut tomatoes in 1/2-inch wedges. Tear lettuce into bite-size pieces; mound on a platter. Alternate strips of cheese, ham and turkey or chicken around center of lettuce. Alternate tomatoes, beets and asparagus around outside of platter. Serve with choice of dressings. Makes 6 servings.

# Blue-Cheese Dressing

*Use as a fresh-vegetable dip.*

1 cup dairy sour cream
2 oz. crumbled blue cheese
1 tablespoon white-wine vinegar

1/8 teaspoon garlic salt
1/8 teaspoon salt

In a small bowl, blend all ingredients. Refrigerate until ready to serve. Makes 1-1/2 cups.

# Quick Thousand-Island Dressing

*Perfect for a seafood salad.*

1/2 cup mayonnaise
1/2 cup dairy sour cream
2 tablespoons chili sauce

1/8 teaspoon salt
Dash of pepper

In a small bowl, blend all ingredients. Refrigerate until ready to serve. Makes 1-1/8 cups.

# Pesto Dressing

*Great as an all-purpose vinaigrette for any salad.*

1/2 cup olive oil
1/4 cup white-wine vinegar
1 garlic clove, crushed

2 tablespoons chopped fresh basil or
  2 teaspoons dried leaf basil
1/4 cup grated Parmesan cheese (3/4 oz.)

Combine all ingredients in a blender or food processor; process until blended. Makes 1 cup.

**Variation**
Substitute 1 tablespoon Dijon-style mustard for Parmesan cheese.

# How to Make Cucumber-Tuna Boats

1/Cut each cucumber in half lengthwise. Using a spoon, scoop out and discard seeds.

2/Drain cucumbers on paper towels. Spoon tuna mixture into cucumber boats.

**8**

# Cucumber-Tuna Boats

*Keep cans of tuna refrigerated so they are cold when you need them in a hurry.*

3 (6- to 8-inch) cucumbers
1 (6-1/2-oz.) can water-pack tuna,
   chilled, drained
2 hard-cooked eggs, chopped

1 medium tomato, seeded, chopped
1/3 cup dairy sour cream
2 tablespoons sweet-pickle relish

Cut each cucumber in half lengthwise. Using a spoon, scoop out and discard seeds. Drain cucumbers, cut-side down, on paper towels. In a medium bowl, combine tuna, eggs, tomato, sour cream and relish. Spoon tuna mixture into cucumber boats. Makes 6 servings.

**15**

# Shrimp-Pasta Salad

*This salad tastes even better the next day.*

8 oz. fettucini
8 oz. cooked baby shrimp
1/2 cup sliced celery

1/4 cup sliced green onions
1/4 cup sliced pitted black olives
Pesto Dressing, opposite

Cook fettucini according to package directions; drain well. Run cold water over cooked fettucini to cool; drain well. Place all ingredients in a large bowl. Toss with dressing. Serve immediately or refrigerate until ready to serve. Makes 6 to 8 servings.

# Smoked-Salmon Salad

*Smoked salmon, though sometimes hard to find, is worth searching out.*

**Creamy Dijon Dressing, see below**
**1 bunch spinach**
**8 oz. fettucini noodles**

**6 oz. smoked or cooked salmon**
**1/4 cup sliced green onions**

*Creamy Dijon Dressing:*
**3/4 cup dairy sour cream**
**1 tablespoon Dijon-style mustard**

**1 tablespoon fresh lemon juice**
**Salt and pepper**

Prepare Creamy Dijon Dressing; set aside. Clean spinach; tear into bite-size pieces. Cook fettucini according to package directions; drain well. Toss hot fettucini with spinach pieces. Run cold water over fettucini mixture to cool; drain well. Place fettucini mixture in a large bowl. Break salmon into bite-size pieces; add to fettucini mixture along with green onions. Toss with Creamy Dijon Dressing. Serve immediately. Makes 4 servings.

**Creamy Dijon Dressing:**
In a small bowl, combine sour cream, mustard and lemon juice; blend well. Season to taste with salt and pepper.

# Far-Eastern Crab Salad

*Treat yourself to a special lunch by trying this salad.*

**6 oz. fresh or frozen crabmeat**
**1/2 cup thinly sliced celery**
**1/4 cup thinly sliced green onions**
**1/3 cup thinly sliced water chestnuts**
**1 (13-1/2-oz.) can pineapple chunks, drained**
**1/2 cup mayonnaise**

**1 tablespoon fresh lemon juice**
**1/2 teaspoon curry powder**
**Curly leaf lettuce**
**1 avocado, sliced**
**1/4 cup slivered almonds**

Break crabmeat into small pieces. In a medium bowl, combine crabmeat, celery, green onions, water chestnuts, pineapple, mayonnaise, lemon juice and curry powder; blend well. Line 4 salad plates or 1 large platter with lettuce. Arrange crab mixture on lettuce. Garnish with avocado slices and almonds. Serve immediately. Makes 4 servings.

# Tomato-Feta Salad

*Feta cheese is a white Greek cheese with a salty flavor.*

**1 pint cherry tomatoes, stems removed**
**2 oz. feta cheese, finely crumbled**

**Pesto Dressing, page 66**

Cut cherry tomatoes in half. In a medium bowl, toss together tomato halves, cheese and dressing. Refrigerate until ready to serve. Makes 4 servings.

# Avocado & Mushroom Vinaigrette

*Mushrooms can marinate overnight if you want to do them ahead.*

1/4 cup olive oil
2 tablespoons fresh lemon juice
1/2 teaspoon dried leaf tarragon
1/4 teaspoon salt

1/8 teaspoon pepper
8 oz. fresh mushrooms, cut in quarters
2 avocados
Curly leaf lettuce

In a small bowl, blend together olive oil, lemon juice, tarragon, salt and pepper. Place mushrooms in a medium bowl. Pour oil mixture over mushrooms; toss to coat well. Refrigerate until ready to serve. To serve, cut avocados in half lengthwise. Peel and remove pits. Arrange lettuce leaves on 4 salad plates; top each with an avocado half. Spoon marinated mushrooms and marinade over each avocado half. Garnish as desired. Serve immediately. Makes 4 servings.

# Tomato-Cheese Vinaigrette

*A beautiful salad to serve on a buffet.*

1 head romaine lettuce
6 large tomatoes, sliced
8 oz. mozzarella cheese, thinly sliced

1 large cucumber, sliced
Pesto Dressing, page 66

Line a round serving plate with romaine leaves, placing stem-end of each leaf in center of plate. Alternate slices of tomato, cheese and cucumber in a circular pattern over lettuce, filling entire plate. Drizzle dressing over top. Refrigerate until ready to serve or serve immediately. Makes 6 servings.

# Cucumbers in Rice Vinegar

*Rice vinegar is a very mild vinegar—perfect for salads.*

2 medium cucumbers
1/4 cup rice vinegar
1/4 cup water

1 teaspoon sugar
1 tablespoon toasted sesame seeds

Score cucumber peeling by running fork tines down the skin. Using a food processor or knife, thinly slice cucumbers. Place cucumber slices in a medium serving bowl. In a small bowl, combine vinegar, water, sugar and sesame seeds. Pour vinegar mixture over cucumbers; toss lightly. Refrigerate until ready to serve. Makes 6 servings.

### Variation

Add 1/2 cup chopped red or green bell pepper to cucumber slices. Proceed as above.

# Tip

*To toast sesame seeds, place in a small skillet over medium heat. Stir constantly until seeds become light brown, 2 to 3 minutes.*

# Warm Potato Salad

*Also tasty served as a cold salad.*

| | |
|---|---|
| **2 lbs. small new red potatoes** | **1 cup coarsely chopped cucumber** |
| **1/2 cup sliced green onions** | **Pesto Dressing, page 66** |

Place a large saucepan of salted water over high heat. Cut unpeeled potatoes into 2-inch cubes; drop into water. Partially cover and bring to a boil. Reduce heat and simmer 10 minutes or until potatoes are tender when pierced with a fork. Place cooked potatoes in a colander. Run cold water over cooked potatoes to cool; drain well. In a large bowl, combine cooked potatoes, green onions and cucumber. Toss with Pesto Dressing. Serve warm. Makes 6 servings.

# Potato Salad with Horseradish Dressing

*A perfect match for hamburgers.*

| | |
|---|---|
| **3 medium potatoes, peeled** | **1 tablespoon prepared horseradish** |
| **4 green onions, chopped** | **Salt and pepper** |
| **1/2 cup mayonnaise** | |

Place a large saucepan of salted water over high heat. Cut potatoes into 2-inch cubes; drop into water. Partially cover and bring to a boil. Reduce heat and simmer 10 minutes or until potatoes are tender when pierced with a fork. Place cooked potatoes in a colander. Run cold water over cooked potatoes to cool; drain well. In a large bowl, combine cooked potatoes, green onions, mayonnaise and horseradish. Season to taste with salt and pepper. Makes 4 servings.

# Antipasto

*Giardinera is mild pickled vegetables, not to be confused with hot pickled vegetables.*

| | |
|---|---|
| **1 (6-oz.) jar marinated artichoke hearts** | **1 (3-oz.) jar small white onions, drained** |
| **1/4 cup white vinegar** | **1 (6-1/2-oz.) can water-pack tuna, drained** |
| **1 (6-oz.) can tomato paste** | **1 (8-oz.) can pitted black olives, drained** |
| **1 (16-oz.) jar Giardinera, drained** | **Salt and pepper** |
| **1 (4-oz.) can button mushrooms, drained** | **1 head lettuce, separated into leaves** |

Drain artichokes, reserving marinade. In a small bowl, combine artichoke marinade, vinegar and tomato paste. In a large bowl, combine Giardinera, mushrooms, onions, tuna and olives. Add marinade mixture; blend well. Season to taste with salt and pepper. Refrigerate until ready to serve. To serve, arrange lettuce leaves on individual plates or 1 large platter. Arrange antipasto on lettuce. Antipasto can be stored in the refrigerator up to 1 week. Also nice served as a side dish on a buffet. Makes 8 servings.

# How to Make Pineapple-Filled Orange Shells

1/Peel pineapple; cut into wedges and then into 1-inch pieces.

2/Cut orange pulp into 1-inch pieces, reserving orange shells.

**12**

## Pineapple-Filled Orange Shells

*Try this for breakfast.*

| | |
|---|---|
| **1 medium, fresh pineapple** | **1 tablespoon finely chopped fresh mint** |
| **4 large oranges** | **8 mint sprigs** |

Peel pineapple; cut into 1-inch pieces. Cut each orange in half crosswise; scoop out orange pulp. Reserve orange-peel shells. Cut pulp into 1-inch pieces. In a small bowl, combine pineapple pieces, orange pieces and chopped mint. Spoon into orange shells. Garnish with mint sprigs. Makes 8 servings.

**9**

## Pineapple-Chili Salad

*An interesting dip served with tortilla chips.*

| | |
|---|---|
| **1 (16-oz.) can crushed pineapple, drained** | **1 cup shredded sharp Cheddar cheese (4 oz.)** |
| **1 (4-oz.) can diced green chilies** | **Lettuce** |
| **2 tablespoons sliced green onion** | **Tortilla chips** |

In a medium saucepan, combine pineapple, chilies, green onion and cheese. Cook over medium-low heat, stirring until cheese melts. Cut lettuce into thin shreds; line 4 salad plates or a large platter with lettuce. Top with tortilla chips. Spoon pineapple mixture over chips. Makes 4 servings.

# Fresh-Fruit Salad   *Photo on page 17.*

*Serve as a light dessert also.*

| | |
|---|---|
| 1 pint fresh strawberries | 3 nectarines, sliced |
| 1 cup plain yogurt (8 oz.) | 1 cup seedless grapes |
| 1 tablespoon brown sugar | 2 bananas, sliced |
| 3 tablespoons orange juice | 1/2 cantaloupe, cut in 1-inch cubes |
| 1 cup fresh blueberries | |

In a medium bowl, crush enough strawberries to measure 1/3 cup. Blend in yogurt, brown sugar and orange juice. Cut remaining strawberries in half, if large. In a serving bowl, combine strawberry halves, blueberries, nectarines, grapes, bananas and cantaloupe. Spoon yogurt mixture over top or serve on the side. Makes 4 to 6 servings.

### Variation

Use frozen unsweetened strawberries, defrosted, and other available fresh fruits, such as oranges, apples, bananas, pineapple or pears.

# Homemade Mayonnaise

*For that extra special touch, make your own mayonnaise.*

| | |
|---|---|
| 1 egg | 1 cup vegetable oil or |
| 1 teaspoon salt, if desired | 1/2 cup vegetable oil and |
| 1/2 teaspoon Dijon-style mustard | 1/2 cup olive oil |
| 1 teaspoon sugar | 1 egg yolk, if needed |
| 1 tablespoon fresh lemon juice | |

In a blender or food processor, combine egg, salt, mustard, sugar and lemon juice. While machine is running slowly, gradually add oil. It should take a full 60 seconds to add all the oil. Turn the machine off; scrape down side of bowl. Process 30 seconds longer. If mayonnaise doesn't thicken, remove from container. Add 1 egg yolk to empty container. With motor running slowly, pour in mayonnaise. Process until thickened. Makes 1-1/2 cups.

### Variations

Add 1 tablespoon chopped fresh dill or 1 teaspoon dill weed.

Add 1 tablespoon chopped fresh tarragon or 1 teaspoon dried leaf tarragon.

**Tartar Sauce:** Add 2 tablespoons sweet-pickle relish and 1/8 teaspoon garlic salt.

# Creamy Parmesan Dressing

*Crisp greens, a little tomato and this dressing are all you need for a perfect salad.*

| | |
|---|---|
| 1 cup dairy sour cream | 2 tablespoons fresh lemon juice |
| 1/4 cup grated Parmesan cheese (3/4 oz.) | 1/8 teaspoon garlic salt |

In a small bowl, blend all ingredients. Refrigerate until ready to serve. Makes 1-1/4 cups.

# Fish & Seafood

Fish is one of the best fast-to-prepare foods available. It is tender, quick to cook and can be used in a variety of ways. There is also a wide variety of seafood products on the market today.

For a casual occasion, serve Halibut en Brochette. Having a more formal function? Serve Champagne-Poached Salmon.

You can easily find seafood that will allow you to prepare it any way you choose—poached, sautéed, broiled or pan-fried. Avoid overcooking any seafood. Serve it immediately after cooking or it may become dry.

With its mild flavor, most seafood combines well with a variety of sauces. Try Oven-Poached Fish with Lemon-Cream Sauce. Or, put seafood in a sauce as in Linguini with Clam Sauce.

When purchasing fish, be sure it is firm to the touch. Avoid fish that is discolored or has an off odor. Remove fish from the package and rinse it in cold water; pat dry with paper towels. Then prepare to cook it. If buying precooked seafood, such as shrimp, place it in ice water with a little lemon juice. Let stand 10 minutes to freshen the flavor.

Fish should be opaque when cooked. To test for doneness, gently flake fish with a fork. Fish usually requires 10 minutes cooking per 1 inch of thickness. Cook frozen fish approximately 20 minutes per inch.

Quick-cooking times for fish provide many interesting opportunities. Try my favorite, Sole en Papillote. Fish fillets are placed in little paper packets along with vegetables and sauce, then sealed and baked. What a perfect entree for a romantic dinner for two! They can also be made ahead for an elegant dinner party.

Newburgs, made from one or several types of seafood, are easy and always delicious. Crab Newburg is an elegant way to stretch crab to feed several people.

Canned fish products are great to keep on the shelf. Canned salmon needs only to have the bones removed to serve or blend into a recipe. It is smart to keep cans of tuna in the refrigerator for a quick already-chilled salad.

**25**

# Catalan Fish in Foil

*A method used in the Spanish province of Catalonia for cooking fish.*

| | |
|---|---|
| 1/2 teaspoon salt | 1/2 large green bell pepper, thinly sliced |
| 1/4 teaspoon pepper | 1-1/2 cups sliced fresh mushrooms |
| 1/8 teaspoon chili powder | 1/3 cup white wine or apple juice |
| 1/4 cup all-purpose flour | 1/4 cup tomato paste |
| 3 lbs. bass fillets | 1 tablespoon minced parsley |
| 1/4 cup olive oil | 1 tablespoon chopped fresh tarragon or |
| 1 garlic clove, minced | 1 teaspoon dried leaf tarragon |

Preheat oven to 425F (220C). Line a 13" x 9" baking pan with a 24-inch piece of foil; let ends hang over. In a pie plate, combine salt, pepper, chili powder and flour; coat fish fillets with mixture. Heat oil in a large skillet. Brown floured fillets in hot oil. Place browned fillets in center of foil. Top with garlic, green pepper and mushrooms. In the large skillet, combine wine or apple juice, tomato paste, parsley and tarragon. Stir briefly over medium heat, scraping the bottom to loosen drippings; spoon mixture over fish. Fold foil over fish; seal edges with a double fold. Bake 15 minutes. Remove from oven; carefully fold back foil over edges of baking dish. Serve immediately. Makes 4 to 5 servings.

**23**

# Fish with Paprika

*Hungarian paprika is available in most large spice departments.*

| | |
|---|---|
| 1 tablespoon butter or margarine | 1/2 cup water |
| 1 medium onion, chopped | 1/2 teaspoon salt |
| 1 tablespoon Hungarian paprika | 1/8 teaspoon pepper |
| 1/8 teaspoon red (cayenne) pepper | 3/4 cup dairy sour cream |
| 2 lbs. sole fillets, cut in serving pieces | |

In a large skillet, melt butter or margarine. Add onion, paprika and red pepper; sauté over medium heat until onion starts to brown. Arrange fish fillets over onion; add water, salt and pepper. Bring to a boil; reduce heat and cover. Cook 5 to 7 minutes or until fish flakes easily with a fork. Place fish on a warm platter; keep warm. Stir sour cream into remaining liquid in skillet; heat to desired serving temperature. Do not boil. Spoon sauce over fish. Makes 4 to 5 servings.

**4**

# Herb-Lemon Butter     *Photo on pages 78 and 79.*

*A good topping for broiled fish.*

| | |
|---|---|
| 1/2 cup butter or margarine, room temperature | 1 tablespoon minced parsley |
| 2 tablespoons fresh lemon juice | 1 tablespoon minced green onion |

In a small bowl, whip butter or margarine, 1 tablespoon lemon juice, parsley and green onion until blended. Gradually beat in remaining lemon juice until fluffy. Refrigerate until ready to use. Makes 3/4 cup.

# Halibut en Brochette

*Photo on pages 78, 79*

**20**

Brochette *means cooked on a skewer.*

2 lbs. halibut steak, cut in 2-inch cubes
8 oz. fresh mushrooms
1 lemon, cut in 1/4-inch slices
1/4 cup butter or margarine, melted

2 teaspoons Dijon-style mustard
2 tablespoons fresh lemon juice
2 tablespoons dry white wine

Preheat broiler or barbecue grill. Alternately thread halibut, mushrooms and lemon slices on 6 metal skewers. In a small bowl, combine butter or margarine, mustard, lemon juice and wine. Brush mixture generously over halibut and mushrooms. Broil or barbecue 4 inches from heat. Brush with marinade; turn after 5 minutes cooking. Cook 5 to 7 minutes longer or to desired doneness. Makes 6 servings.

# Turbot in Orange-Butter Sauce

**23**

*Turbot pinwheels are an attractive way to serve thin fillets.*

2 lbs. turbot fillets
1/2 cup butter
1/2 cup orange juice

2 teaspoons grated orange peel
1/2 teaspoon salt
1/8 teaspoon pepper

Preheat oven to 450F (230C). Grease an 11" x 7" baking dish; set aside. Cut each fillet in half lengthwise. Roll each piece and secure with wooden picks, if needed. Arrange rolled fillets in greased baking dish. In a small saucepan, melt butter; stir in orange juice, orange peel, salt and pepper. Pour mixture over fish. Cover with foil. Bake 15 minutes or until fish flakes easily with a fork. Makes 6 servings.

# Oven-Poached Fish with Lemon-Cream Sauce

**25**

*If fish fillets are 1/2 inch thick or less, fold in half before poaching.*

1-1/2 to 2 lbs. (1-inch-thick)
  halibut fillets
1 cup clam juice
3 lemon slices

1 parsley sprig
1 cup whipping cream
1 teaspoon grated fresh lemon peel
2 tablespoons dry white wine

Preheat oven to 400F (205C). Place fish in an 11" x 7" baking pan. Pour clam juice over fish; top with lemon slices and parsley. Cover tightly with foil. Bake 10 to 20 minutes. Fish should be opaque and flake easily with a fork. To prepare sauce, pour cooking liquid into a small saucepan. Bring liquid to a boil; boil quickly to reduce by 1/2. Add whipping cream, lemon peel and wine. Cook until slightly thickened, stirring frequently. Serve over fish. Makes 4 to 6 servings.

## Tip

*Broil, fry or barbecue fish 10 minutes for every 1 inch of thickness. If fish is frozen, double cooking time.*

# How to Make Sole en Papillote

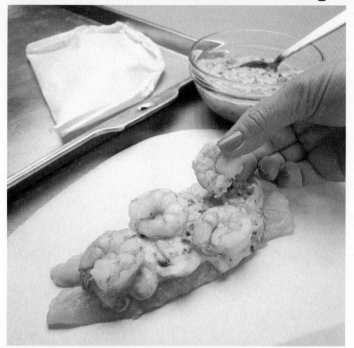

1/Arrange fish on parchment paper; top with sauce. Arrange shrimp over sauce.

2/Serve packets directly on a plate, garnished with a fresh herb sprig.

**25**

## Sole en Papillote

*Serve fish attractively in individual parchment-paper packages.*

2 tablespoons butter or margarine
2 tablespoons dry white wine
1 medium bay leaf
1 cup thinly sliced fresh mushrooms
1/4 cup chopped green onions
2 tablespoons chopped fresh parsley
2 tablespoons all-purpose flour

1/4 teaspoon salt
1/8 teaspoon white pepper
1/3 cup milk
4 (8-oz.) sole, flounder, red-snapper or
   seabass fillets
8 oz. peeled, cooked medium shrimp

Preheat oven to 425F (220C). To prepare sauce, in a medium saucepan, melt butter or margarine. Add wine, bay leaf, mushrooms, green onions and parsley; sauté 1 minute. Stir in flour, salt and white pepper. Add milk, stirring constantly, until mixture comes to a boil and thickens. Remove and discard bay leaf. To make papillotes, cut 4 (15" x 11") hearts from parchment paper. Place a fish fillet on 1 side of each paper heart. Spoon sauce evenly over fillets. Top each with 4 to 5 shrimp. Fold paper over fillet so edges meet. Starting at top end, fold edges over twice to crimp, down to pointed end. Repeat with remaining papillotes. Place papillotes on a baking sheet. Bake 10 to 12 minutes or until paper begins to turn golden. To serve, make an X-shape cut in top of each packet. Pull parchment back to expose fish. Place each packet on a plate. Serve immediately. Makes 4 servings.

On following pages: Quick Brie Spread with apples, page 42; Halibut en Brochette, opposite; Curry-Green-Pea Salad, page 64; Peach-Macaroon Melba, page 134; Herb-Lemon Butter, page 75; and Lemonade Rosé, page 151.

# South of the Border Clams

*Serve as an appetizer or main dish.*

24 fresh unopened clams
2 tablespoons olive oil
1 medium onion, chopped
1 garlic clove, minced

1 (6-oz.) can tomato paste
1 (8-oz.) bottle clam juice
1/2 teaspoon dried leaf oregano
3 drops hot-pepper sauce

Place clams in a large bowl of salted water; let stand 10 minutes to clean out any sand. In a large Dutch oven, heat oil. Add onion and garlic; sauté until onion is transparent. Stir in tomato paste, clam juice, oregano and hot-pepper sauce. Place clams in Dutch oven. Cover and cook 10 minutes over medium heat. Discard any clams that do not open. Makes 3 to 4 servings.

# Linguini with Clam Sauce

*Frozen chopped clams are the best choice, but canned clams will work nicely.*

8 oz. linguini
1/2 cup olive oil
3 tablespoons butter or margarine
1 medium onion, chopped
2 garlic cloves, minced

1 lb. chopped clams with juice
2 tablespoons chopped fresh basil or
   2 teaspoons dried leaf basil, crumbled
1/4 cup minced parsley
Grated Parmesan cheese

Cook linguini according to package directions; drain well. Keep linguini hot. Meanwhile, in a large skillet, heat oil and butter or margarine. Add onion and garlic; sauté over medium heat 1 to 2 minutes. Stir in clams, basil and parsley. Heat to desired serving temperature. Serve clam sauce over hot linguini. Sprinkle cheese on top. Makes 4 servings.

# Shrimp-Spaghetti Italiano

*An economical way to serve shrimp.*

8 oz. spaghetti
1/4 cup olive oil
1/2 cup butter or margarine
8 oz. uncooked medium shrimp, shelled,
   deveined, cut in half lengthwise
2 garlic cloves, minced
1/2 medium onion, chopped
1/2 cup sliced pimiento-stuffed green olives

1/4 cup minced parsley
1/2 cup coarsely chopped walnuts
1 tablespoon fresh lemon juice
1/2 teaspoon salt
1/8 teaspoon pepper
1/4 teaspoon dried leaf basil
1/4 teaspoon dried leaf oregano
Grated Parmesan cheese

Cook spaghetti according to package directions; drain well. Keep spaghetti hot. Meanwhile, in a large skillet, heat oil and butter or margarine. Add shrimp, garlic and onion; sauté until shrimp turns pink. Add olives, parsley, walnuts, lemon juice, salt, pepper, basil and oregano. Heat thoroughly; then toss with hot spaghetti. Serve with cheese. Makes 4 servings.

# How to Make Chinese Tuna Rolls

1/Spoon tuna mixture evenly over center of tortilla; fold and roll tortilla.

2/Slide each rolled tortilla into an onion ring; garnish with a green-onion fan.

**15**

# Chinese Tuna Rolls

*Serve this over rice instead of wrapped in tortillas.*

2 tablespoons butter or margarine
1 medium onion, chopped
1 cup diagonally sliced celery
3 (6-1/2-oz.) cans water-pack tuna, drained
1 (10-oz.) pkg. frozen chopped spinach,
    thawed, well drained
1-1/2 cups sliced fresh mushrooms
1 (8-oz.) can water chestnuts, drained,
    thinly sliced

1/4 cup cornstarch
3 cups chicken broth or stock
2 tablespoons soy sauce
1 tablespoon prepared mustard
1/2 teaspoon salt
12 (8-inch) flour tortillas
2 red onions, sliced in 1/4-inch rings
12 green-onion fans, page 12 and 13

Melt butter or margarine in a large skillet. Add onion and celery; sauté until tender. Add tuna, spinach, mushrooms and water chestnuts; cook 2 minutes. In a small bowl, blend cornstarch and about 1/4 cup broth or stock; stir mixture into tuna mixture along with remaining broth or stock. Add soy sauce, mustard and salt. Cook, stirring constantly, over medium heat until mixture boils and thickens. Spread tortillas on a flat surface. Spoon tuna mixture evenly over center of each tortilla. Roll tortilla, enclosing filling; slide into an onion ring or secure with a wooden pick. Garnish with a green-onion fan. Repeat with remaining tortillas. Makes 12 tortilla rolls or 6 servings.

**15**

# Fettucini with Shrimp

*Fresh or homemade noodles really do make a taste difference.*

1 (8 oz.) pkg. fettucini
1/4 cup butter or margarine
8 oz. small whole fresh mushrooms
8 oz.. uncooked medium shrimp, shelled,
   deveined

1 garlic clove, crushed
1/4 cup dry white wine
1 cup whipping cream

Cook fettucini according to package directions; drain well. Keep pasta hot. Melt butter or margarine in a large skillet. Add mushrooms, shrimp and garlic; sauté until shrimp turns pink and mushrooms are cooked. Add wine and whipping cream. Bring to a simmer. Serve over hot fettucini. Makes 4 servings.

**15**

# Scallops Giovani

*A favorite way to serve scallops.*

1 (8-oz.) pkg. spinach fettucini or
   spiral noodles
2 tablespoons butter or margarine
1 medium onion, chopped
1 green bell pepper, cut in 1/4-inch strips
3 cups sliced fresh mushrooms

2 cups coarsely chopped fresh tomatoes
1 lb. small bay scallops or
   large scallops cut in quarters
1 cup dairy sour cream
1/4 cup dry white wine
1/2 cup grated Parmesan cheese (1-1/2 oz.)

Cook pasta according to package directions; drain well. Keep pasta hot. Meanwhile, melt butter or margarine in a large skillet. Add onion and bell pepper; sauté until onion is transparent. Add mushrooms, tomatoes and scallops. Cook 3 to 5 minutes or until scallops are cooked through. Blend in sour cream and wine. Heat until warm through. Toss scallop mixture with fettucini. Makes 4 servings.

**14**

# French Scallops

*Scallops have such a delicate taste, they need only a small amount of added flavoring.*

1/4 cup butter
1/4 cup chopped green onions
1 tablespoon chopped fresh dill
1/4 teaspoon salt

1/8 teaspoon hot-pepper sauce
1 lb. scallops
2 tablespoons dry white wine

In a chafing dish or large skillet, melt butter over medium heat. Add green onions, dill, salt and hot-pepper sauce. Cook until mixture bubbles. Then add scallops. Cook, stirring occasionally, until scallops are tender, 5 to 8 minutes. Add wine; cook 2 minutes longer. Makes 4 servings.

# Crab Newburg

Newburg *means cooked with a sauce made of egg yolks, cream, sherry and butter.*

| | |
|---|---|
| 1 (6- to 8-oz.) pkg. fresh or<br>    frozen king crabmeat | 1/4 teaspoon paprika |
| 1/4 cup butter or margarine | 1-1/4 cups half and half |
| 2 tablespoons all-purpose flour | 3 egg yolks |
| 1/8 teaspoon salt | 3 tablespoons dry sherry |
| | 4 baked puff-pastry shells or cooked rice |

Defrost and drain frozen crabmeat. Cut crabmeat into 1/2-inch pieces. Melt butter or margarine in a medium saucepan over medium heat. Stir in flour, salt and paprika. In a medium bowl, beat together half and half and egg yolks; pour into saucepan. Stir over medium heat until mixture thickens. Add crab and sherry; heat to desired serving temperature. Serve in puff-pastry shells or over rice. Makes 4 servings.

### Variation

Substitute shrimp or any combination of shrimp, crab, scallops or firm white fish for crabmeat.

# Crab Brunch Scramble    Photo on page 17.

*For a festive midday brunch, feature colorful crab in a creamy egg dish.*

| | |
|---|---|
| 1 (6- to 8-oz.) pkg. fresh or<br>    frozen king crabmeat | 1/2 cup dairy sour cream |
| 1/4 cup butter | 2 tablespoons grated Parmesan cheese |
| 2 tablespoons sliced green onion | 1 teaspoon salt |
| 8 eggs, slightly beaten | 1/8 teaspoon pepper |
| | 3 English muffins, split, toasted, buttered |

Defrost and drain frozen crab. Break crab into bite-size pieces. In a medium skillet, melt butter. Add green onion; sauté over medium heat 1 to 2 minutes. In a medium bowl, beat together eggs, sour cream, cheese, salt and pepper. Add egg mixture and crabmeat to green onion; cook, stirring constantly, until partially set. To serve, spoon cooked egg mixture over toasted muffin halves. Makes 3 to 6 servings.

# Deluxe Shrimp & Eggs

*This dish makes a good midnight supper.*

| | |
|---|---|
| 8 oz. peeled, cooked shrimp | 1/4 teaspoon paprika |
| 3 bacon slices | 6 eggs, beaten |
| 1/3 cup chopped onion | 1/4 cup half and half |
| 1/2 cup chopped green bell pepper | 1/2 teaspoon Worcestershire sauce |
| 1/2 teaspoon salt | |

Cut large shrimp in half lengthwise; set aside. In a 9-inch skillet, fry bacon until crisp; remove bacon, reserving drippings. Drain bacon; then crumble. Sauté onion and green pepper in bacon drippings until tender. Add salt, paprika and shrimp; heat. In a medium bowl, combine eggs, half and half, Worcestershire sauce and crumbled bacon. Pour egg mixture into skillet with shrimp mixture. Cook until eggs are firm, stirring occasionally. Makes 6 servings.

**30**

# Jambalaya

*This is my version of a Southern favorite.*

3/4 lb. hot Italian sausage, casings removed
2 onions, chopped
1 green bell pepper, chopped
1 garlic clove, minced
2 (16-oz.) cans tomatoes
2 cups chicken broth or stock

1 tablespoon Worcestershire sauce
1/2 teaspoon dried leaf thyme
8 oz. uncooked shrimp, shelled, deveined
1 cup diced cooked chicken or turkey
1/4 teaspoon hot-pepper sauce

In a large skillet, sauté sausage and onions over medium heat until sausage is cooked and crumbly. Drain off excess fat. Add green pepper and garlic; sauté 1 minute. Add tomatoes with juice, broth or stock, rice, Worcestershire sauce and thyme. Bring to a boil. Reduce heat and cover; simmer 15 minutes. Add shrimp, chicken or turkey, and hot-pepper sauce. Cook 5 minutes longer or until rice is tender and shrimp are pink. Makes 6 servings.

**10**

# Shrimp Sauté

*Shrimp tastes outstanding cooked in this manner.*

1/2 cup butter or margarine
1 garlic clove, crushed
1-1/2 lbs. uncooked shrimp, shelled,
  deveined

1 tablespoon minced parsley
1 cup dry white wine
Juice of 1 lemon
1/4 teaspoon Worcestershire sauce

In a large skillet, melt butter or margarine with garlic. Add shrimp; sauté 3 minutes. Add parsley, wine, lemon juice and Worcestershire sauce. Heat 2 minutes longer. Makes 4 servings.

**15**

# Shrimp in Beer

*Be sure to set out a large bowl for shrimp shells.*

2 (12-oz.) cans flat beer
1 medium onion, sliced
1 garlic clove, crushed
Juice of 1 lemon

1/4 teaspoon black peppercorns
1/2 cup chopped celery leaves
2 lbs. uncooked medium shrimp
1 cup butter, melted

In a large pot, combine beer, onion, garlic, lemon juice, peppercorns and celery leaves. Cover and bring to a boil; reduce heat and simmer 5 minutes. Add shrimp. Reduce heat and simmer 3 to 5 minutes or until shrimp turn pink. Do not overcook after adding shrimp because they will become tough. Drain shrimp. Serve with melted butter for dipping. Makes 4 servings.

# *How to Make Champagne-Poached Salmon*

1/Using a wooden pick, secure narrow ends of each salmon steak.

2/Poach salmon in champagne mixture until salmon flakes easily with a fork.

**20**

# *Champagne-Poached Salmon*

*Serve leftover salmon chilled with a vinaigrette sauce for a change.*

**4 cups champagne**
**1 lemon, thinly sliced**
**1 teaspoon black peppercorns**
**2 whole allspice or**
   **1/4 teaspoon ground allspice**

**1 teaspoon dill weed**
**4 (1/2- to 3/4-inch-thick) salmon steaks**
**1 cup whipping cream**

In a large skillet, combine champagne, lemon, peppercorns, allspice and dill weed. Bring to a boil; reduce heat. Using a wooden pick, secure narrow ends of each salmon steak. Arrange salmon in champagne mixture. Cover and poach 10 minutes or until salmon flakes easily with a fork. Remove salmon; place on a warm platter. Bring poaching liquid to a boil; boil quickly to reduce by 1/2. Add whipping cream; bring to a simmer. Stirring constantly, reduce sauce slightly. Serve over salmon. Makes 4 servings.

# Poultry

Poultry, whether it be chicken, turkey or Cornish hen, is one of the most versatile meats. Its natural tenderness and moistness are perfect for fast-cooking meals. The meat has a mild flavor that blends well with other flavors, including a wide variety of herbs and spices.

Poultry is very economical. You can use all parts with minimal waste. Parmesan Chicken Wings is a perfect example. Even the wing-tips can be simmered in a saucepan of water with vegetables for a tasty chicken stock.

Broiling is a favorite method for cooking chicken parts. It gives the chicken skin a nice crisp texture and adds to the overall flavor. Try serving broiled Dijon Chicken for rave reviews. Skin can be removed before cooking, if desired. However, check during cooking to insure that the meat doesn't dry out. You may need to brush chicken pieces with butter, margarine or a favorite marinade to keep it moist and flavorful.

Sautéing or stir-frying is a fast-to-fix method for cooking boneless poultry. Pieces hold their shape while cooking so they look neat and uniform when served. Pineapple-Glazed Chicken is a quick and delicious stir-fry recipe.

On chicken packages, the term *broiler-fryer* means it is an all-purpose bird that can be broiled, baked, sautéed, roasted or simmered. These birds are young, tender and meaty.

When buying chicken, figure on three pounds for four servings, allowing about 3/4 pound per serving. Boneless poultry yields two to three servings per pound. Small Cornish hens can be served whole. If large, split hens in half for each serving.

Poultry can be stored in the refrigerator for up to two days after it is purchased. For longer storage, rewrap tightly in moisture- and vapor-proof paper suitable for freezing. Uncooked poultry can be frozen at 0F (20C) up to 12 months if properly wrapped. Cooked poultry can be frozen six months without losing its flavor.

Cooked poultry products are also quick and easy to prepare. When roasting or boiling poultry, prepare extra. Then cut the cooked poultry in small cubes and freeze for future use. It is especially convenient to have cooked poultry to use when you need a meat dish on a moment's notice. Turkey Tetrazzini is a good example of quick cooking using cooked poultry. Any poultry can be substituted for the turkey.

With a little imagination, you will be amazed at the versatility of poultry in 30-minute-meal plans. 🌺

---

## Swiss Chicken

*Perfect party fare.*

6 (1/2-inch-thick) French-bread slices
6 (1/8-inch-thick) Swiss-cheese slices
1/4 cup butter or margarine
6 boneless chicken-breast halves, skinned
1/2 cup dry white wine

8 oz. fresh mushrooms, sliced
2 tablespoons all-purpose flour
1 cup milk
1/4 teaspoon salt

Preheat oven to 325F (165C). Arrange bread slices on a baking sheet; place a slice of cheese on each bread slice. Place in oven to melt cheese. In a large skillet, melt butter or margarine. Add chicken pieces; cook until done. Place 1 piece cooked chicken on top of each bread slice. Return to oven to keep warm. Pour wine into same skillet. Add mushrooms; sauté until cooked. Stir in flour, milk and salt. Cook, stirring constantly, until slightly thickened. Place chicken-topped bread on a platter. Top with mushroom sauce. Makes 6 servings.

## Chicken with Lemon-Cream Sauce

*A touch of lemon gives the sauce a delicious flavor.*

6 tablespoons butter or margarine
2 tablespoons fresh lemon juice
4 boneless chicken-breast halves, skinned
1-1/2 cups sliced fresh mushrooms

1 tablespoon cornstarch
3/4 cup chicken broth or stock
1 cup whipping cream

In a large skillet, melt 3 tablespoons butter or margarine. Stir in 1 tablespoon lemon juice. Add chicken pieces; cook over medium heat until lightly browned. Remove to a warm platter; cover with foil to keep warm. In same skillet, melt remaining 3 tablespoons butter or margarine. Stir in 1 tablespoon lemon juice and mushrooms; sauté until slightly cooked. In a small bowl, dissolve cornstarch in broth or stock. Stir cornstarch mixture and cream into mushrooms. Cook 2 to 3 minutes or until slightly thickened. Do not boil. Pour sauce over cooked chicken. Makes 4 servings.

# Florentine Chicken

*Florentine in a recipe title means the dish includes spinach.*

6 boneless chicken-breast halves, skinned
6 tablespoons butter or margarine
1/4 cup white wine
1 medium onion, chopped
8 oz. fresh mushrooms, sliced
2 bunches spinach

2 tablespoons all-purpose flour
1 cup milk
1/4 teaspoon salt
1/8 teaspoon pepper
1 cup shredded Swiss cheese (4 oz.)

Cut 2 chicken pieces in half. Melt 2 tablespoons butter or margarine in a large skillet. Add wine and all chicken pieces; cook until done. Remove from skillet; keep warm. In same skillet, melt 2 tablespoons butter or margarine. Add onion and mushrooms; sauté until onion is transparent. Place spinach leaves on top. Cover and cook over medium-low heat 5 minutes. In a small saucepan, melt 2 tablespoons butter or margarine. Stir in flour; cook 1 minute. Add milk, salt and pepper, stirring until slightly thickened. Stir in cheese until sauce is smooth. Preheat broiler. Divide spinach mixture between 4 ovenproof ramekins. Place 1-1/2 cooked chicken pieces in each ramekin on top of spinach mixture. Pour cheese sauce over all. Broil, 6 inches from heat, 4 minutes or until sauce is lightly browned. Makes 4 servings.

# Dijon Chicken

*Simple but oh so tasty!*

1/3 cup Dijon-style mustard
1 tablespoon chopped green onion
Salt

Pepper
Garlic salt
1 (3- to 4-lb.) chicken, cut in pieces

Preheat broiler; grease broiler pan. In a small bowl, combine mustard and green onion. Sprinkle salt, pepper and garlic salt over chicken pieces. Place chicken pieces, skin-side down, on broiler pan. Broil, 6 inches from heat, 10 minutes. Turn chicken; brush with mustard mixture. Broil 10 minutes longer or until done. Makes 4 servings.

# Yakitori

*A Japanese-style chicken barbecue on skewers.*

4 boneless chicken-breast halves, skinned
3/4 cup soy sauce
1/4 cup saké or dry sherry

2 teaspoons sugar
1/2-inch piece fresh gingerroot,
   thinly sliced, if desired

Cut chicken in 1-inch squares. Thread chicken pieces onto skewers. In a medium saucepan, combine soy sauce, saké or dry sherry, sugar and gingerroot, if desired. Bring to a boil; reduce heat and simmer 15 minutes. Preheat broiler or prepare barbecue grill. Brush each skewer of chicken with soy-sauce mixture. Cook, 4 inches from heat, 2 to 3 minutes; turn and brush with sauce. Cook 2 minutes longer or until done. Brush with sauce; place on a platter. Makes 4 servings.

 **Tip**

*If using bamboo skewers, soak in water before cooking to prevent burning.*

# *How to Make Italian Chicken Supreme*

1/Roll chicken pieces, enclosing ham, cheese and herb sprig. Secure with a wooden pick.

2/Fry chicken until light brown on all sides. Garnish with additional herb sprigs.

**15**

## *Italian Chicken Supreme*

*Fresh breadcrumbs are made easily in a food processor or blender.*

**4 boneless chicken-breast halves, skinned**
**2 thin slices sandwich ham, cut in half**
**4 oz. mozzarella cheese, cut in 4 slices**
**4 (1-inch) fresh sage or dill sprigs**
**1/2 cup all-purpose flour**

**1 egg, beaten**
**1-1/2 cups fresh breadcrumbs**
**Oil for frying**
**Additional herbs, if desired**

Arrange each chicken piece between 2 pieces waxed paper; pound with a mallet or rolling pin to flatten to about 1/4 inch thick. Place a piece of ham on top of each chicken piece. Add a cheese slice and sage or dill sprig to each chicken piece. Roll up each chicken piece half-way; fold in sides, envelope-style, and continue rolling. Secure with a wooden pick. Roll each chicken piece in flour, then in beaten egg, then in breadcrumbs. Pour oil to a 1-inch depth in a large skillet. Heat to 365F (185C) or until a 1-inch cube of bread turns golden brown in 60 seconds. Fry chicken until light brown on all sides, about 5 minutes. Garnish with herbs, if desired. Makes 4 servings.

### Variation

**Mushroom Filling:** Prepare a mushroom stuffing to use in place of ham and cheese slices. Melt 2 tablespoons butter or margarine in a large skillet. Add 1/4 cup chopped onion and 1/2 cup chopped fresh mushrooms; sauté until all liquid has evaporated. Divide mixture evenly between flattened chicken-breast halves. Roll up. Cook as above.

# Pineapple-Glazed Chicken

*Pork is a good substitute for chicken; cooking time will be slightly longer.*

1 lb. boneless uncooked chicken
2 tablespoons vegetable oil
1/2 green bell pepper, cut in 1-inch pieces
1/2 medium onion, cut in 1/2-inch slices
1 (8-oz.) can pineapple slices

2 tablespoons soy sauce
1 tablespoon saké or dry sherry
1 tablespoon cornstarch
Polka-Dot Rice, page 116, or
   other cooked rice

Cut chicken in 1-inch pieces to make about 1-1/2 cups chicken. Heat oil in a large skillet. Add chicken pieces; sauté 2 minutes. Add green pepper and onion; stir-fry until chicken is tender. Drain pineapple, reserving juice. Cut pineapple into 1-inch wedges. In a small bowl, combine reserved pineapple juice, soy sauce, saké or dry sherry and cornstarch; pour over chicken. Stir-fry until sauce has thickened slightly and chicken and vegetables are well coated. Serve over rice. Makes 6 servings.

# Turkey Tetrazzini

*For a richer sauce, substitute half and half for milk.*

1 (8-oz.) pkg. spinach noodles
1/4 cup butter or margarine
1/2 medium onion, cut in 1/2-inch strips
1/2 cup thinly sliced carrots
1 cup fresh broccoli flowerets
8 oz. fresh mushrooms, sliced

1/4 cup all-purpose flour
1/2 teaspoon salt
1/8 teaspoon pepper
1/4 teaspoon ground nutmeg
1 pint milk (2 cups)
3 cups diced cooked turkey (about 1 lb.)

Cook noodles according to package directions; drain well. Keep noodles warm. Meanwhile, in a large skillet, melt butter or margarine. Add onion, carrots and broccoli; sauté until tender. Add mushrooms; cook 1 minute. Stir in flour, salt, pepper and nutmeg until blended. Add milk; stir until thickened. Add turkey; cook 5 minutes or to desired serving temperature. Serve over hot cooked noodles. Makes 6 servings.

# Baked Chicken Wings

*Chicken wings make great appetizers, too!*

2/3 cup grated Parmesan cheese (2 oz.)
2 tablespoons all-purpose flour
1 teaspoon ground sage

1 cup milk
2 lbs. chicken wings, wing-tips removed

Preheat oven to 425F (220C). Place a rack on a 15" x 10" baking sheet. In a heavy-duty plastic bag, combine cheese, flour and sage. Pour milk into a shallow bowl. Dip wing pieces in milk; then shake in bag of seasoning mix to coat completely. Place seasoned wings on rack, 1 layer deep. Bake 20 minutes or until done. Makes 6 servings or 10 appetizer servings.

# How to Make Parmesan Chicken Wings

1/Cut wings at each joint, discarding wing-tips or save for other use.

2/Dip wing pieces in milk; shake in cheese mixture to coat well.

**15**

## Parmesan Chicken Wings

*A strong pair of kitchen scissors makes cutting wing joints easy.*

2 lbs. chicken wings
1/2 cup grated Parmesan cheese (1-1/2 oz.)
1/4 cup all-purpose flour
1 teaspoon dried leaf oregano, crumbled

1/2 teaspoon salt
1/4 teaspoon pepper
1 cup milk

Preheat broiler; grease broiler pan. Cut wings at each joint, discarding wing-tips or save for other use. In a heavy-duty plastic bag, combine cheese, flour, oregano, salt and pepper. Pour milk into a shallow bowl. Dip wing pieces in milk; then shake in cheese mixture to coat completely. Place seasoned wing pieces on greased pan. Broil, 4 inches from heat, 7 minutes; turn and broil 5 minutes longer or until done. Makes 6 dinner servings or 10 appetizer servings.

# Country-Style Cornish Hens

*Use a strong pair of kitchen scissors to cut hens in half or have your butcher do it.*

1/2 cup all-purpose flour
1/4 teaspoon salt
1/8 teaspoon pepper
1/4 teaspoon dried leaf oregano, crumbled
1/8 teaspoon ground sage
2 Cornish hens, cut in half
2 tablespoons vegetable oil

1 small onion, sliced
1/2 medium eggplant, cut in 1-inch cubes
1 red or green bell pepper,
　cut in 1/2-inch strips
4 oz. fresh mushrooms, sliced
1 carrot, cut in 1/8-inch slices

In a heavy-duty plastic bag, combine flour, salt, pepper, oregano and sage. Shake each hen half in flour mixture until evenly coated. Heat oil in a large skillet. Add floured hen halves; cook until browned on both sides. Remove browned hen halves from skillet; set aside. To skillet, add onion, eggplant, red or green pepper, mushrooms and carrot. Sauté vegetables 3 minutes. Place browned hen halves on top of vegetables. Cover and simmer 15 minutes or until done. Makes 4 servings.

# Mandarin Cornish Hens

*Cornish hens are always a special treat.*

3 Cornish hens, cut in half
1 (8-oz.) can mandarin-orange segments
1/4 cup butter or margarine, melted
3/4 cup orange juice
1/2 teaspoon salt

1/4 cup sugar
1 tablespoon cornstarch
3/4 cup dry white wine
1 teaspoon grated orange peel
1/8 teaspoon ground ginger

Preheat broiler. Place hens, breast-side down, on a rack in a broiler pan. Drain orange segments, reserving juice. In a small bowl, combine 2 tablespoons reserved juice, butter or margarine, 1/4 cup orange juice and salt; spoon mixture over hens. Broil, 6 inches from heat, 10 minutes. Turn hens; baste well. Cook 10 to 12 minutes longer or until done. Meanwhile, in a small saucepan, combine sugar and cornstarch. Stir in remaining reserved juice, 1/2 cup orange juice, white wine, orange peel and ginger. Bring to a boil, stirring constantly. When thickened, stir in orange segments; heat through. Serve sauce over Cornish hens. Makes 6 servings.

**Variation**

If Cornish hens are small, allow 1 per serving.

**Tip**

*For thickening, 1 tablespoon cornstarch has the same thickening capacity as 2 tablespoons flour. Cornstarch will give a clear appearance to a sauce. Flour gives a creamy appearance.*

# Beef, Pork, Lamb & Veal

Beef is the main item in a majority of dinner menus across the country. Rightfully so, because it is nutritious, available in a variety of cuts and is tender and tasty.

Many beef cuts can be prepared with quick-cooking methods. Stir-Fry Americana uses the stir-fry technique to seal in the delicious flavor and quickly cook both meat and vegetables. Classic Steak with Green Peppercorns has a distinct flavor. This is perfect for any special occasion. Oven-Baked Meatballs can be made ahead and frozen. When ready to serve, top with Quick Sweet & Sour Sauce.

Veal is very young and tender. Although costly and sometimes difficult to find, it is well worth the search. It has a delicate flavor. My favorite way to prepare veal is Veal with Zucchini & Dill. Veal chops or cutlets are sautéed lightly, then topped with dill-flavored zucchini rounds. Veal Piccata, another tasty dish, is sautéed and then given a splash of fresh lemon juice for added flavor. When preparing veal, remember that overcooking will toughen the meat.

Over the past few years, leaner pork has been available. That's due to research and modern production techniques. For you, that means delicious pork flavor with fewer calories.

Fresh and cured pork combine well with a variety of herbs, spices and other flavorings. Pork can often be substituted for poultry or beef in recipes. Try Monterey Steak made with a thick pork chop and see what I mean. Cooked pork can be substituted for turkey in Turkey Tetrazzini, page 91, for a new and different flavor combination.

When cooking fresh pork, it is important to cook it to an internal temperature of 170F (75C). Fully cooked pork products should be cooked to an internal temperature of 140F (60C). Uncooked ham should be cooked until it reaches 160F (70C).

Lamb is gaining in popularity. Today's lamb is very young and tender, with a light flavor. The two most common cuts are lamb chops and leg of lamb. Ground lamb is available in some areas. Try ground lamb in Burgundy-Spinach Burgers. Lamb can be served rare, depending on personal preference.

Imagination is essential in meat cookery. Adapt favorite recipes to quick-cooking techniques and create new favorites. Use precooked meat to create high-protein, fast-cooking dishes that are sure to please all. ❧

---

# Orange-Mint Lamb Chops

*Mint is the perfect taste accent for lamb.*

1/4 cup chopped fresh mint or
  1 tablespoon dried leaf mint,
  crumbled
1/4 cup orange marmalade

2 tablespoons mint jelly
1 tablespoon cider vinegar
6 lamb shoulder chops

Preheat broiler. In a small saucepan, combine mint, marmalade, jelly and vinegar. Heat slightly to melt jelly, stirring to blend. Place lamb chops on a broiler pan; brush top side with marmalade mixture. Broil, 6 inches from heat, 6 to 8 minutes. Turn and brush with marmalade mixture. Broil 6 to 8 minutes longer or to desired doneness. Makes 6 servings.

# Quick Chutney-Sauced Lamb Chops

*If you love chutney sauce, you'll enjoy these lamb chops.*

6 lamb loin chops
1/3 cup orange juice

1 teaspoon cornstarch
1/2 cup chutney, finely chopped

Preheat broiler. Broil lamb chops, 6 inches from heat, 5 to 6 minutes per side for medium-well done. In a small saucepan, combine orange juice and cornstarch; stir in chutney. Cook until slightly thickened, stirring constantly. Serve with broiled lamb chops. Makes 4 to 6 servings.

# Lamb & Vegetable Kabobs

*Kabobs can be assembled the night before; then covered and refrigerated until ready to cook.*

1/2 cup olive oil
1 garlic clove, crushed
1/4 teaspoon dried leaf basil, crumbled
1/4 teaspoon dried leaf oregano, crumbled
2 tablespoons lemon juice

1-1/2 lbs. boneless lamb, cut in
  2-inch cubes
1 small eggplant, cut in 2-inch cubes
2 tomatoes, cut in quarters
2 ears of corn, cut in 3 pieces each

Preheat broiler. In a small bowl, combine oil, garlic, basil, oregano and lemon juice. Alternate pieces of lamb, eggplant, tomatoes and corn on 6 metal skewers. Brush kabobs with oil mixture. Broil kabobs, 6 inches from heat, 7 minutes. Turn and brush with oil mixture. Broil 7 to 10 minutes longer or to desired doneness. Makes 6 servings.

# Monterey Steak

*Steak covered with mushrooms — a perfect combination.*

1-1/2 lbs. beef top-sirloin steak
3 tablespoons butter or margarine
1 tablespoon Worcestershire sauce
1 teaspoon dried leaf basil, crumbled
1/2 teaspoon dried leaf tarragon, crumbled
3 cups sliced fresh mushrooms

1/2 cup dry white wine
1/4 teaspoon salt
1/8 teaspoon pepper
1 cup shredded Monterey Jack cheese (4 oz.)
1 tablespoon all-purpose flour

Cut beef in 4 serving pieces. In a large skillet, melt butter or margarine. Add Worcestershire sauce, basil and tarragon. Place beef in skillet; cook 5 minutes on each side for medium-rare. Remove to a warm platter; cover with foil to keep warm. Place mushrooms in skillet. Add wine, salt and pepper; sauté until mushrooms are cooked. In a small bowl, toss cheese with flour; stir into mushrooms. Cook until cheese is melted. Pour mushroom sauce over steaks. Serve immediately. Makes 4 servings.

# Sukiyaki

*Cook at the serving table in an electric wok or electric skillet.*

1/2 cup soy sauce
1/4 cup sugar
1 cup beef stock or broth
1/2 head Chinese cabbage,
    cut into 1/4-inch-wide slices
1 bunch spinach
10 green onions, cut in 1-inch pieces
1 large onion, sliced

12 fresh mushrooms, sliced
8 oz. tofu (bean curd),
    cut in 1/2-inch cubes
1 cup fresh bean sprouts
1 lb. beef sirloin steak, thinly sliced
3 tablespoons vegetable oil
Cooked rice

In a small bowl, combine soy sauce, sugar and stock or broth. Arrange cabbage, spinach, green onions, sliced onion, mushrooms, tofu, bean sprouts and beef separately on a large platter. In a wok or large skillet, heat oil over high heat. Add beef; brown slightly. Add remaining ingredients from platter. Pour in soy-sauce mixture. Stir-fry 5 minutes or until beef and vegetables are cooked to desired doneness. Serve immediately with rice. Makes 4 to 6 servings.

# Green-Chili Stroganoff

*A Tex-Mex twist to an old favorite.*

2 tablespoons vegetable oil
1 lb. beef sirloin steak,
   cut in 1/8-inch-thick strips
1 medium onion, sliced
1 garlic clove, minced
1-1/2 cups sliced fresh mushrooms
1 (7-oz.) jar salsa or 1 cup Salsa,
   page 45

1 (4-oz.) can diced green chilies
1/2 teaspoon chili powder
1/4 cup dry red wine
1/2 teaspoon salt
1/8 teaspoon pepper
1 cup dairy sour cream
Cooked rice

In a large skillet, heat oil over high heat. Add beef strips, onion, garlic and mushrooms; sauté until beef is browned. Stir in salsa, chilies, chili powder, wine, salt, pepper and sour cream. Reduce heat; cook until mixture reaches serving temperature. Do not boil. Serve over rice. Makes 4 to 6 servings.

# Beef Stroganoff

*Stroganoff, named after its inventor, is a Russian method of serving beef.*

1 lb. beef sirloin steak
2 tablespoons vegetable oil
1 small onion, sliced
3 cups sliced fresh mushrooms
1/2 cup red wine
1 garlic clove, crushed
1 cup beef broth or stock

1 teaspoon prepared mustard
2 tablespoons ketchup
1/2 teaspoon salt
1/8 teaspoon pepper
1 cup dairy sour cream
Cooked noodles or rice

Cut beef in 1/4-inch-thick strips. In a large skillet, heat oil. Add beef strips and onion; brown lightly. Add mushrooms, wine and garlic; sauté 2 minutes. Stir in broth or stock, mustard, ketchup, salt and pepper. Cover and simmer 10 minutes. Stir in sour cream. Serve immediately over noodles or rice. Makes 4 servings.

# Classic Steak with Green Peppercorns

*Green peppercorns come packed in brine and are found in gourmet food shops.*

2 tablespoons butter or margarine
2 (8- to 12-oz.) beef sirloin steaks
1/3 cup finely chopped onion
1/4 cup brandy

1 tablespoon green peppercorns or capers,
   drained
3/4 cup whipping cream
1 tablespoon Dijon-style mustard

In a large skillet, melt butter or margarine. Add steaks; cook over high heat 3 minutes on each side for medium-rare. Cook longer for a more well-done steak. Place steaks on a warm platter; cover with foil to keep warm. Reduce heat. Add onion; sauté until transparent. Add brandy; scrape brown particles from bottom of pan. Add peppercorns or capers; crush with the back of a spoon. Stir in cream and mustard. Bring mixture to a simmer, stirring until slightly thickened. Pour sauce over steaks. Serve immediately. Makes 2 servings.

# How to Make Beef & Vegetable Roll

1/On a large piece of plastic wrap, form ground beef into a 7-inch square. Arrange cooked vegetables across beef. Sprinkle with cheese.

2/Using plastic wrap and your hands, gently roll meat beginning with a side parallel to vegetables; pinch to seal edges.

**25**

# Beef & Vegetable Roll

*Colorful vegetables inside make a pretty surprise.*

| | |
|---|---|
| **1 zucchini** | **2 green onions** |
| **1 carrot** | **1 lb. lean ground beef** |
| **1 celery stalk** | **1 oz. crumbled blue cheese** |

Preheat broiler. Cut zucchini, carrot and celery into 6-inch-long narrow strips. Cut green onions into 6-inch pieces. In a 10-inch skillet, pour water to a 2-inch depth. Bring water in skillet to a boil; add vegetable pieces. Boil 1 to 2 minutes or until vegetables are slightly tender; drain well. On a 12-inch length of plastic wrap, form ground beef into a 7-inch square. Arrange cooked vegetables lengthwise down center of meat. Top with cheese. Using plastic wrap, gently roll up meat beginning with a side parallel to vegetables. Remove plastic wrap; pinch edges of meat together as a seal. Place beef roll on broiler pan. Broil, 4 inches from heat, about 5 minutes. Gently roll meat over to opposite side. Broil 5 minutes longer. Turn beef 1/2 turn, if needed, to brown all sides. Remove from heat. Let stand 5 minutes; then slice into 4 (1-1/2-inch-thick) slices. Makes 4 servings.

**20**

# Oven-Baked Meatballs

*Freeze leftover meatballs for future use.*

| | |
|---|---|
| 1 lb. lean ground beef | 1 teaspoon salt |
| 1 egg | 1 teaspoon dried minced onion |
| 2 tablespoons regular or | 1 teaspoon dried leaf oregano, crumbled |
| quick-cooking rolled oats | 1 tablespoon Dijon-style mustard |

Preheat oven to 500F (260C). In a large bowl, combine all ingredients. Using a teaspoon or melon baller, shape beef mixture into 1-inch balls; drop on a 15" x 10" jelly-roll pan. Bake uncovered 5 to 7 minutes. Makes approximately 40 meatballs.

**15**

# Burgundy-Spinach Burgers

*Serve these burgers with Quick Tomato-Corn Relish, page 119.*

| | |
|---|---|
| 1 (10-oz.) pkg. frozen chopped spinach, thawed | 1/4 cup grated Parmesan cheese (3/4 oz.) |
| | 1/2 small onion, chopped |
| 1-1/2 lbs. ground beef | 1 teaspoon salt |
| 1/4 cup red wine | 1/8 teaspoon pepper |

Preheat broiler. Squeeze spinach to remove excess liquid. In a large bowl, combine all ingredients until well blended. Form into 6 patties. Broil, 6 inches from heat, about 5 minutes on each side for medium-rare or to desired doneness. Makes 6 servings.

**25**

# Sicilian Meatball Soup

*Mini-meatballs are quick to make by scooping them out with a teaspoon or melon baller.*

| | |
|---|---|
| 1 egg | 1/2 teaspoon salt |
| 1 lb. ground beef | 1/8 teaspoon pepper |
| 1/2 cup soft white breadcrumbs (1 slice) | 9 cups beef broth or stock |
| 2 tablespoons finely chopped parsley | 4 oz. thin egg noodles |
| 2 tablespoons grated Parmesan cheese | Additional Parmesan cheese |
| 1 small garlic clove, crushed | |

In a medium bowl, beat egg slightly. Add ground beef, breadcrumbs, parsley, 2 tablespoons Parmesan cheese, garlic, salt and pepper; blend well. Using a teaspoon or melon baller, shape meat mixture into approximately 40 small balls. In a 6-quart saucepan, bring broth or stock to a boil. Gradually add meatballs. Stir gently to separate. Simmer meatballs 5 minutes. Using a slotted spoon, remove meatballs; set aside. Bring broth or stock to a boil; add noodles. Cook 5 to 7 minutes, stirring occasionally. Return meatballs to broth or stock; cook 5 minutes longer or until noodles are tender. Serve with additional Parmesan cheese to sprinkle on top. Makes 8 servings.

# How to Make Stir-Fry Americana

1/Cut vegetables in thin slices for fast, even cooking and an attractive appearance.

2/Stir-fry meat and vegetables 2 to 3 minutes or until tender.

**18**

# Stir-Fry Americana

*Slicing vegetables on the diagonal exposes more surface to absorb flavors and cook faster.*

3 tablespoons vegetable oil
1 lb. beef round steak, cut in
   1/8-inch-wide strips
1-1/2 cups diagonally cut
   (1/8-inch-thick) carrots
1 cup (1/8-inch-thick) sliced cauliflowerets
6 oz. fresh or frozen pea pods
1 (10-oz.) pkg. frozen whole-kernel corn

1 medium onion, cut in 1/8-inch slices
1-1/2 cups sliced fresh mushrooms
1/4 cup soy sauce
1 tablespoon dry sherry
1/2 teaspoon ground ginger
1/2 cup cold water
2 tablespoons cornstarch

Heat oil in a wok or large skillet. Add beef and carrots; stir-fry until beef has browned. Add cauliflower, pea pods, corn, onion and mushrooms; stir-fry 2 to 3 minutes or until tender. In a small bowl, combine soy sauce, sherry, ginger, water and cornstarch. Add to meat and vegetables; stir to coat each piece well. Cook 3 to 4 minutes longer to thicken sauce. Makes 6 servings.

## Liver au Gratin

*Liver prepared a way most everyone will enjoy it.*

| | |
|---|---|
| 1/4 cup butter or margarine | 1 (6-oz.) pkg. sliced Monterey Jack cheese |
| 1 medium onion, sliced | 1/2 cup dry sherry |
| 8 oz. fresh mushrooms, cut in quarters | 1/2 teaspoon dried leaf rosemary, crumbled |
| 1 lb. sliced calves' liver | 1/2 teaspoon dried leaf basil, crumbled |

In a large skillet, melt butter or margarine. Add onion and mushrooms; sauté over medium heat until onion is transparent. Remove from skillet; set aside. In the same skillet, fry liver over medium heat until brown on both sides. Top each liver piece with a slice of cheese. Add sherry, rosemary, basil and sautéed onion and mushrooms. Cover and simmer 10 minutes. Makes 4 servings.

## Quick Sweet & Sour Sauce

*Use this sauce when stir-frying pork and vegetables.*

| | |
|---|---|
| 1/4 cup cider vinegar | About 1/2 cup pineapple juice |
| 1 tablespoon cornstarch | 1/2 cup packed brown sugar |

In a small saucepan, combine vinegar, cornstarch, 1/2 cup pineapple juice and brown sugar. Bring to a boil, stirring constantly; reduce heat. Simmer 5 minutes. If sauce is too thick, add a little pineapple juice. Makes 1 cup.

## Quick Béarnaise Sauce

*A perfect sauce to make in the microwave.*

| | |
|---|---|
| 4 oz. whipped cream cheese | 1 tablespoon minced onion |
| 2 egg yolks | 2 tablespoons white wine |

In a small saucepan, combine all ingredients. When blended, heat slowly over low heat, stirring constantly, until hot. Do not boil. Makes 1/2 cup.

**Variation**

**To microwave:** In a glass bowl, heat cream cheese on full power (HIGH) 1 minute. Stir in remaining ingredients.

# Veal with Zucchini & Dill

*A tasty dish for that special occasion.*

| | |
|---|---|
| 3 tablespoons butter or margarine | 1/4 teaspoon salt |
| 4 (6-oz.) veal chops or cutlets | Pepper |
| 2 medium zucchini, sliced | 1 tablespoon fresh lemon juice |
| 1 medium onion, sliced | |
| 1 tablespoon chopped fresh dill or | |
|    1 teaspoon dill weed | |

In a large skillet, melt butter or margarine. Add veal; cook over medium heat to desired doneness. Place veal on a warm platter; cover with foil to keep warm. In the same skillet, sauté zucchini, onion and dill until tender. Season to taste with salt, pepper and lemon juice. Spoon zucchini mixture over warm veal. Makes 4 servings.

### Variation

To make a cream sauce, after sautéing zucchini, add 1 cup whipping cream. Bring to a simmer. Season to taste with salt, pepper and lemon juice. Serve as above.

# Veal Piccata

*Veal and chicken are interchangeable in many recipes, including this one.*

| | |
|---|---|
| 4 (6-oz.) veal chops or cutlets | 3 tablespoons fresh lemon juice |
| 1/2 cup all-purpose flour | Salt and pepper |
| 6 tablespoons butter | 1 tablespoon chopped fresh parsley |
| 1/3 cup dry white wine | |

Coat veal on each side with flour. In a large skillet, melt butter. Add floured veal; cook over medium-low heat 5 minutes, turning to brown both sides lightly. Add wine and lemon juice. Season with salt and pepper. Cover and simmer 5 minutes or until veal is done. Place on a warm platter. Pour pan drippings over veal. Sprinkle parsley over top. Makes 4 servings.

# Sausage-Stuffed Apples

*A nice accompaniment for ham or pork chops.*

| | |
|---|---|
| 1 lb. breakfast sausage | 1/4 cup raisins |
| 2 tablespoons chopped onion | 1/4 teaspoon ground cinnamon |
| 4 medium cooking apples | 1/8 teaspoon ground nutmeg |

Preheat oven to 400F (205C). Grease an 8-inch-square baking pan. In a medium skillet, cook sausage and onion until sausage is no longer pink. While sausage is cooking, cut a 1/2-inch slice from top of each apple; remove and discard core. Scoop out and reserve apple pulp, leaving a 1/2-inch shell. Chop apple pulp; add to sausage mixture along with raisins, cinnamon and nutmeg. Blend well. Cook until hot. Place apples in greased pan. Spoon sausage mixture into apples. Place remaining sausage mixture in bottom of pan. Cover tightly with foil. Bake 20 minutes or until apples are tender. Makes 4 servings.

**28**

# Ginger-Glazed Pears & Ham

*With the many varieties of fresh pears available throughout the year, you can prepare this dish anytime.*

| | |
|---|---|
| 3 fresh pears | 2 tablespoons water |
| Fresh lemon juice | 2 tablespoons fresh lemon juice |
| 1 (1-1/2-inch-thick) fully cooked ham slice (about 2 lbs.) | 1 tablespoon butter |
| | 1 teaspoon ground ginger |
| 1/2 cup packed brown sugar | 1 teaspoon prepared mustard |

Preheat oven to 350F (175C). Core pears; cut each in 8 wedges. Dip pear wedges in lemon juice to prevent discoloration. Place ham slice on a rack in a shallow baking pan; arrange pear wedges around ham. Bake 10 minutes. Meanwhile, in a small saucepan, combine brown sugar, water, 2 tablespoons lemon juice, butter, ginger and mustard. Simmer 5 minutes or until slightly syrupy. Remove ham from oven; brush glaze over ham and pears. Bake 10 minutes longer. Remove ham slice to a platter; arrange pear wedges around ham. Pour remaining glaze over ham. Makes 6 servings.

**14**

# Ham & Asparagus with Curry Sauce

*These bundles are nice for a buffet.*

| | |
|---|---|
| 1 lb. fresh or frozen asparagus spears, cooked | 1/4 cup all-purpose flour |
| | 1/2 teaspoon curry powder |
| 4 thin slices cooked ham | 1 pint milk (2 cups) |
| 1/4 cup butter or margarine | 1/4 teaspoon salt |
| 1/2 onion, finely chopped | 1/8 teaspoon pepper |

Preheat broiler. Arrange asparagus in 4 piles; cut so all spears are approximately the same length. Wrap each bundle in a ham slice; secure with a wooden pick, if necessary. Place on a broiler pan; broil, 6 inches from heat, 5 minutes or until desired serving temperature. Meanwhile, in a medium saucepan, melt butter or margarine. Add onion; sauté over medium heat until soft. Stir in flour and curry powder. Blend in milk. Stir over medium heat until thickened. Add salt and pepper. Arrange warm asparagus bundles on a platter. Pour sauce over bundles. Serve immediately. Makes 4 servings.

**25**

# Apricot-Honey-Glazed Ham

*Partially cutting the ham into serving slices speeds up baking time.*

| | |
|---|---|
| 1 (2-lb.) boneless ham | 1/4 teaspoon ground cinnamon |
| 1/4 cup raisins | 1/4 cup honey |
| 1 (5-1/4-oz.) can apricot nectar | 5 whole cloves |

Preheat oven to 350F (175C). Cutting 3/4 the way through, cut ham into 6 equal slices. Place ham in an 8-inch-square baking dish. In a small saucepan, combine raisins, apricot nectar, cinnamon and honey; bring to a boil. Place 1 clove between each ham slice to hold slices apart. Pour apricot glaze over ham. Bake 20 minutes, occasionally basting with glaze. Makes 6 servings.

**27**

# Pork Fried Rice

Stir-fry *means to stir food quickly as it cooks over high heat.*

3 cups water
1/4 cup soy sauce
1-1/2 cups uncooked long-grain white rice
1/2 teaspoon salt
2 tablespoons vegetable oil
6 green onions, cut in
    1-inch diagonal pieces

2 cups diagonally sliced celery
10 fresh mushrooms, thinly sliced
1/2 cup diced green or red bell pepper
1 (8-oz.) can water chestnuts, sliced
1 cup diced cooked pork

In a medium saucepan, combine water and soy sauce; bring to a boil. Add rice and salt. Cover and cook over medium heat until rice has absorbed all water and is tender, about 20 minutes. In a wok or large skillet, heat oil over high heat. Add green onions, celery, mushrooms, green or red pepper and water chestnuts; stir-fry 2 minutes. Add cooked rice and pork; stir-fry 3 minutes or to desired serving temperature. Makes 6 servings.

**Variation**

**Chicken Fried Rice:** Substitute 1 cup diced cooked chicken for pork.

**28**

# Cassoulet

*A quick version of a classic dish from southern France.*

2 bacon slices, minced
1/2 lb. boneless pork, cut in
    1/2-inch cubes
1 onion
6 whole cloves
1/2 lb. boneless lamb, cut in
    1/2-inch cubes
1 garlic clove, minced

2 Italian sausages, cut in
    1/4-inch slices
1 teaspoon salt
1/4 teaspoon pepper
1/4 teaspoon dried leaf thyme
2 (16-oz.) cans white beans, undrained
1 (16-oz.) can tomato sauce

In a large skillet or Dutch oven, sauté bacon and pork until pork is tender. Cut onion in 6 wedges; insert a clove in each onion wedge. Add onion wedges, lamb, garlic and sausage to pork mixture; sauté until lamb is tender. Add salt, pepper, thyme, beans and tomato sauce. Cover and simmer 15 minutes. Makes 4 to 6 servings.

**25**

# Curried Pears

*Delicious served with lamb, pork or poultry.*

2 tablespoons butter, room temperature
3 tablespoons brown sugar

1/2 teaspoon curry powder
1 (29-oz.) can pear halves, drained

Preheat oven to 350F (175C). In a small bowl, combine butter, brown sugar and curry powder. Arrange pears, flat-side up, in a shallow baking dish. Sprinkle butter mixture over pears. Bake 20 minutes. Makes 4 to 6 servings.

# How to Make Yam-Stuffed Pork Roast

1/Spoon about 1/4 cup yam mixture over each of 5 chops. Stack chops evenly, one on top of the other.

2/Push skewers through all chops from top to bottom to secure together. Place in a roasting pan.

**30**

## Yam-Stuffed Pork Roast

*Pork chops skewered together make an easy-to-serve roast.*

3 tablespoons butter or margarine
6 (3/4-inch-thick) smoked pork chops
1 large apple, chopped
1 (16-oz.) can yams, drained, chopped

1/4 cup raisins
1/4 cup orange juice
1/4 teaspoon ground cinnamon

Preheat oven to 375F (190C). In a large skillet, melt butter or margarine. Add chops; brown on both sides. Remove chops. In the same skillet, sauté apple until slightly soft. Stir in yams, raisins, orange juice and cinnamon; warm through. To assemble roast, spoon about 1/4 cup yam mixture over each of 5 chops. Stack chops evenly, 1 on top of the other, forming a roast. Top with remaining plain chop. Push skewers through all chops from top to bottom to secure together. Place in a roasting pan. Cover with foil; bake 20 minutes or until warm through. Makes 4 to 6 servings.

**25**

# Pork Chops à L'Orange

*Pork and orange make a tasty combination.*

2 tablespoons vegetable oil
6 pork shoulder chops
1/2 teaspoon salt
1/8 teaspoon pepper
1 cup orange juice
1/4 teaspoon ground ginger
1/4 teaspoon ground nutmeg

1/4 teaspoon dry mustard
1/2 teaspoon dried leaf marjoram
1 tablespoon grated orange peel
1 tablespoon cornstarch
2 tablespoons water
1 small orange, thinly sliced

In a large skillet, heat oil over medium heat. Add pork chops; brown chops on both sides. Sprinkle salt and pepper over browned chops. In a small bowl, combine orange juice, ginger, nutmeg, mustard, marjoram and orange peel; pour over chops. Cover and simmer 15 minutes. Place chops on a platter; cover with foil to keep warm. In a small bowl, combine cornstarch and water; pour into cooking liquid in skillet. Cook over high heat, stirring constantly, until thickened. Pour thickened sauce over chops. Garnish with orange slices. Makes 6 servings.

**18**

# Squash Medley with Smoked Pork Chops

*Smoked pork chops have a similar flavor to ham and are easy to prepare.*

2 tablespoons butter
6 smoked pork chops (about 3 lbs.)
1 medium zucchini, thinly sliced
2 crookneck squash, thinly sliced

1 medium onion, thinly sliced
2 teaspoons dill weed
1/2 cup shredded Cheddar cheese (2 oz.)

Melt butter in a large skillet. Add pork chops; brown on each side 5 minutes to heat through. Place chops on a warm platter; cover with foil to keep warm. In the same skillet, add zucchini, crookneck squash, onion and dill weed; sauté over high heat, stirring constantly, until squash is tender. Spoon squash mixture over chops; immediately sprinkle cheese over squash. Heat from the vegetables will slightly melt cheese by the time you are ready to serve. Makes 4 to 6 servings.

**25**

# Choucroute Garnie

*A traditional dish from Alsace, but served all over France.*

1 lb. apple sausage or
 other sausage variety
4 bacon slices, chopped
1 cup apple juice

1 tablespoon brown sugar
1 tablespoon cider vinegar
4 cups sauerkraut, rinsed, drained well
1 teaspoon caraway seeds

Score sausage at 1-inch intervals. In a large skillet, sauté bacon; drain off fat. Add sausage and apple juice; cover and simmer 10 minutes. Stir in brown sugar and vinegar. Add sauerkraut. Sprinkle caraway seeds on top. Cover and simmer 10 minutes to heat through and blend flavors. Makes 4 servings.

# Vegetables

Good year-round availability of fresh vegetables has put them on everyone's list of favorites. Bright colors and varying tastes make for interesting cooking combinations. Vegetables are versatile. They can be stir-fried, sautéed, steamed or baked. The quickest cooking methods are steaming, sautéing and stir-frying.

**Steaming** is one of the fastest and most nutritious ways to cook vegetables. Purchase a steaming rack that will fit inside a covered saucepan. Pour a small amount of water in the bottom of the saucepan. Put the rack in the saucepan. Place vegetables on the rack. Cover and bring to a gentle boil. Vegetables are cooked by steam from the boiling water. Vegetables should not touch the water. Steaming times will vary with individual vegetables and how thick they are cut.

**Sautéing** is a fast method of cooking that seals in delicious flavors. Quickly cooking the vegetables in hot butter, margarine or oil gives a different taste. Herbs can be added to give a distinct flavor. Stirring frequently prevents vegetables from sticking to the skillet.

**Stir-frying** is similar to sautéing. It can be done in a wok or skillet. Meat is often added to stir-fried vegetables to make a one-dish meal. Cook meat in a small amount of oil over high heat. Then add vegetables. It is important to stir constantly to cook each piece evenly. When combining different types of vegetables, the dense, more firm-textured vegetables, such as onions, carrots and cauliflower, should be cooked first. Then, add those vegetables that cook quickly, like tomatoes, mushrooms and bean sprouts. That way, all vegetables are cooked to perfection at the same time.

When buying vegetables, look for quality and freshness, especially if you are buying a three- to four-day supply. Know your market well. When I buy vegetables and fruits at a produce market, I know they will stay fresh three to five days longer than if I purchase them at my local supermarket. Bright, true colors and a clean fresh smell mean good quality. Avoid vegetables that are limp, decaying or smell musty. Vegetables at their peak season will usually be the best-dollar value. Out-of-season vegetables will be more costly and often less tasty.

If you cannot get the type or quality of fresh vegetables you need, try using their frozen counterpart. Frozen spinach is a timesaver. When used in a recipe, it tastes much like fresh spinach. Frozen broccoli spears are nice for a year-round attractive green vegetable. Frozen corn-on-the-cob is a real treat in the middle of winter. Avoid overcooking vegetables because they lose their bright colors easily.

Think of serving vegetables for all meals during the day. As a breakfast dish, try Spinach Italiano. Eggplant Parmigiana is a light luncheon dish, side dish or dinner entree.

When preparing vegetables for cooking or serving raw, cut them into interesting shapes. If you always cut zucchini into round slices, try spears. Or, if you usually cut green beans in 2-inch pieces, try leaving them whole. Serving different shapes makes a more interesting dish. One type of vegetable used in a recipe should be cut the same for even cooking.

With today's emphasis on high fiber and light meals, vegetable dishes are very popular. Combine them with cheese or a cream sauce and they become a well-balanced meal in themselves. 🐝

---

## Spinach-Topped Artichoke Hearts

*Use whipped cream cheese when blending it by hand with other ingredients.*

2 (10-oz.) pkg. frozen chopped spinach,
  thawed
1 (6-oz.) jar marinated artichoke hearts,
  drained
1 (8-oz.) pkg. cream cheese,
  room temperature

2 tablespoons butter or margarine,
  room temperature
1/4 cup milk
1/2 cup grated Parmesan cheese (1-1/2 oz.)

Preheat oven to 350F (175C). Grease a 1-quart casserole. Drain spinach well, squeezing out excess moisture. Place artichoke hearts in bottom of greased casserole; pat spinach over artichoke hearts. In a food processor or by hand, blend cream cheese, butter or margarine, milk and Parmesan cheese. Spread cheese mixture evenly over spinach. Cover with lid or foil. Bake 10 minutes. Remove cover; bake 10 minutes longer. Makes 6 servings.

## Stir-Fried Asparagus

*Any fresh vegetable or vegetable combination works well with this sauce.*

2 lbs. fresh asparagus or
  3 (10-oz.) pkgs. frozen asparagus,
  thawed
1 tablespoon vegetable oil
1 tablespoon cornstarch

1 cup chicken broth or stock
2 tablespoons soy sauce
1 garlic clove, crushed
1/2 cup thinly sliced water chestnuts

Cut asparagus into 2-inch diagonal pieces. In a wok or large skillet, heat oil. Add asparagus pieces; stir-fry 1 minute. In a small bowl, combine cornstarch, broth or stock, soy sauce and garlic; pour over asparagus. Add water chestnuts. Stir-fry 3 minutes or until sauce is thickened and asparagus is tender. Makes 6 servings.

# Sweet & Sour Baked Beans

*Butter beans and green beans add freshness and color.*

1 onion, finely chopped
4 bacon slices, cut in 1-inch pieces
1/4 cup cider vinegar
1/2 cup packed brown sugar
1/2 teaspoon garlic powder

1 teaspoon salt
1/4 teaspoon pepper
1 (10-oz.) pkg. frozen butter beans
1 (16-oz.) can kidney beans
1 (10-oz.) pkg. frozen green beans

In a large skillet, cook onion and bacon until bacon is crisp; drain off all but 1 tablespoon drippings. To skillet, add vinegar, brown sugar, garlic powder, salt and pepper; blend well. Add butter beans, kidney beans and green beans. Cover and simmer 15 minutes, stirring occasionally to prevent sticking. Makes 6 to 8 servings.

# Skillet-Baked Beans

*Molasses is the ideal way to sweeten baked beans for that real homemade flavor.*

3 bacon slices
1 medium onion, sliced
3 (16-oz.) cans baked beans

1/3 cup ketchup
1/4 cup molasses
2 teaspoons Worcestershire sauce

In a large skillet, sauté bacon and onion 5 minutes or until onion is golden. Add baked beans, ketchup, molasses and Worcestershire sauce. Simmer 15 to 20 minutes, stirring frequently. Makes 8 servings.

# Horseradish-Creamed Beets

*Delicious served with roast beef.*

1 (16-oz.) can small round beets
1/2 cup dairy sour cream

2 tablespoons prepared horseradish
1/4 cup sliced green onions

Drain and rinse beets. In a medium bowl, combine sour cream, horseradish and green onions. Stir in drained beets. Refrigerate until ready to serve. Makes 2 cups.

# Broccoli Supreme

*Sour-cream sauce is also good over green beans.*

2 lbs. fresh broccoli, trimmed, or
    2 (10-oz.) pkgs. frozen broccoli spears
1 cup dairy sour cream

2 tablespoons dry onion-soup mix
2 tablespoons dry sherry

Steam fresh broccoli until tender or cook frozen broccoli according to package directions. In a small saucepan, combine sour cream, onion-soup mix and sherry. Heat over low until hot. Do not boil. Place cooked broccoli on a platter. Top with warm sauce. Makes 4 to 6 servings.

# Deluxe Broccoli

*Try serving this delicious sauce over Brussels sprouts or califlower.*

1-1/2 to 2 lbs. fresh broccoli, trimmed, or
   2 (10-oz.) pkgs. frozen broccoli spears
2 tablespoons butter or margarine
1/2 cup chopped onion
2 tablespoons all-purpose flour

1/4 teaspoon salt
Dash of pepper
1 cup dairy sour cream
1/2 cup shredded Cheddar cheese (2 oz.)

Steam fresh broccoli or cook frozen broccoli according to package directions. In a small saucepan, melt butter or margarine. Add onion; sauté over medium heat. Stir in flour, salt, pepper and sour cream. Simmer to warm through. Do not boil. Arrange cooked broccoli in a serving dish. Pour sour-cream sauce over broccoli; sprinkle cheese over top. Makes 4 to 6 servings.

# Sautéed Cabbage & Apples

*Great to serve with broiled pork chops.*

1/4 cup butter or margarine
2 large apples, finely chopped
3 cups thinly sliced cabbage
1/2 onion, finely chopped
1/2 teaspoon salt

1/4 teaspoon ground nutmeg
1/4 cup cider vinegar
1 tablespoon sugar
1/3 cup chopped walnuts

Melt butter or margarine in a large skillet. Add apples, cabbage, onion, salt, nutmeg, vinegar and sugar; sauté until cabbage and apples are tender. Stir in nuts. Cook 2 minutes. Makes 4 servings.

# Pineapple-Glazed Carrots

*Carrots never tasted so good.*

1 lb. carrots, thinly sliced
1 (8-1/4-oz.) can pineapple tidbits
   with juice

1/2 cup water
1/4 cup orange juice

In a medium saucepan, combine all ingredients. Bring to a boil over medium heat. Cover and simmer 7 minutes or until carrots are tender. Makes 4 servings.

# Fluted Carrot Coins

*Fluted vegetable cutters have a zig-zag blade that makes an attractive cut.*

8 medium carrots
1/2 cup beef broth or stock

Using a fluted vegetable cutter or paring knife, cut carrots in 1/8-inch-thick slices. In a medium saucepan, combine sliced carrots and broth or stock. Bring to a boil; reduce heat and simmer 7 minutes or until carrots are tender. Makes 4 to 6 servings.

# How to Make Mustard Cauliflower

1/Line a saucepan with cheesecloth so ends come up the side. Place cauliflower on top of cheesecloth.

2/Pour mayonnaise mixture over cooked cauliflower. Sprinkle cheese over sauce.

**25**

## Mustard Cauliflower

*This is the only way my family will eat cauliflower.*

1 medium cauliflower
3/4 cup mayonnaise
2 tablespoons minced green onion

1 teaspoon prepared mustard
1/2 cup shredded Cheddar cheese (2 oz.)

Remove outer cauliflower leaves; trim core, leaving cauliflower whole. In a large saucepan, bring 2 cups water to a boil. Add whole cauliflower. Cover and cook 20 minutes or until tender when pierced with a fork. Meanwhile, in a small saucepan, combine mayonnaise, green onion and mustard. Cook over low heat until warm. Place cooked cauliflower on a plate or shallow dish. Pour mayonnaise sauce over cooked cauliflower. Sprinkle cheese over sauce. Makes 4 to 6 servings.

## Tip

*For easy preparation of whole cauliflower, line a saucepan with a large piece of cheesecloth so that ends come up the pan side and over the edge. Place cauliflower in saucepan on top of cheesecloth. Place lid on so it holds cheesecloth from slipping inside. Trim cheesecloth so it doesn't hang down near the burner. When cauliflower is cooked, use cheesecloth to lift it from the pan.*

# Eggplant Parmigiana

*Eggplant can be prepared unpeeled or peeled as a matter of personal preference.*

| | |
|---|---|
| Tomato Sauce, see below | Salt and pepper |
| 1 medium eggplant | 1/2 cup grated Parmesan cheese (1-1/2 oz.) |
| 1/4 cup olive oil | 1 (8-oz.) pkg. sliced mozzarella cheese |

*Tomato Sauce:*

| | |
|---|---|
| 2 tablespoons olive oil | 1 (6-oz.) can tomato paste |
| 1/2 cup finely chopped onion | 1 (16-oz.) can tomatoes, cut up |
| 1/4 cup finely chopped celery | 1/2 teaspoon dried leaf oregano |
| 1/2 garlic clove, minced | 1/2 teaspoon dried leaf basil |

Preheat broiler. Grease an 11" x 7" baking pan; set aside. Prepare Tomato Sauce. Slice eggplant in round 1/2-inch-thick slices. Brush oil over each slice; sprinkle salt and pepper over oiled slices. Arrange eggplant slices on a broiler pan in a single layer. Broil, 4 inches from heat, 3 minutes. Turn slices; broil 3 minutes longer. Reduce oven to 400F (205C). Place 1/2 the broiled eggplant slices in greased baking pan to cover bottom. Sprinkle 1/2 the Parmesan cheese over top. Pour 1/2 the Tomato Sauce over top. Add 1/2 the mozzarella cheese. Repeat with remaining eggplant, Parmesan cheese, Tomato Sauce and mozzarella cheese. Bake 5 minutes or until warm through. Makes 4 to 6 servings.

**Tomato Sauce:**

Heat oil in a medium saucepan. Add onion, celery and garlic; sauté until onion is transparent. Stir in tomato paste, tomatoes with juice, oregano and basil. Simmer over medium heat 5 minutes.

**Variation**

Substitute 2 to 3 thinly sliced zucchini for eggplant.

# Spinach Italiano

*Serve this with poached eggs for a breakfast treat.*

| | |
|---|---|
| 1 lb. Italian sweet sausage, casings removed | 1 teaspoon dried leaf oregano, crumbled |
| 1/2 medium onion, chopped | 2 bunches spinach |
| 1-1/2 cups sliced fresh mushrooms | 1/4 cup dry white wine |
| 1/2 teaspoon garlic salt | Dairy sour cream |

In a large skillet, sauté sausage, onion, mushrooms, garlic salt and oregano. When sausage is no longer pink, pour off excess fat. Meanwhile, clean and trim spinach; tear into bite-size pieces. Add spinach and wine to cooked sausage mixture; steam 3 to 4 minutes or until spinach has wilted. Stir to blend mixture. Serve with sour cream as a topping. Makes 4 to 6 servings.

 **Tip**

*One pound fresh spinach equals about 1 cup cooked spinach.*

**12**

# Pineapple & Pea Pods Exotica

*An exotic sweet-and-sour blend of fruit and vegetables.*

2 tablespoons butter or margarine
1/4 teaspoon curry powder
1/4 cup sliced green onions
8 oz. fresh or frozen pea pods
1 (8-1/4-oz.) can pineapple chunks
1 tablespoon cornstarch

1 tablespoon brown sugar
1 tablespoon cider vinegar
1/2 cup chicken broth or stock
2 teaspoons soy sauce
1 tomato, cut in 8 wedges
1/4 cup sliced water chestnuts

In a medium skillet, melt butter or margarine until bubbly. Stir in curry powder. Add green onions and pea pods. Cook, stirring constantly, 2 minutes. Drain pineapple, reserving 1/4 cup juice. In a small bowl, combine 1/4 cup pineapple juice, cornstarch, brown sugar, vinegar, broth or stock and soy sauce; add to pea-pod mixture. Cook, stirring constantly, until sauce becomes clear. Stir in tomato, water chestnuts and drained pineapple chunks. Cook until all ingredients are hot. Makes 4 to 5 servings.

**24**

# Sautéed Pepper Strips

*Serve as a colorful, tasty side dish or as a cold salad.*

3 green, red or yellow bell peppers or
 a combination
3 tablespoons olive oil

1/4 teaspoon dried leaf oregano
Salt and pepper

Cut peppers into 1/2-inch-wide strips. In a medium skillet, heat oil. Add pepper strips and oregano; sauté over low heat 15 to 20 minutes or until tender. Season to taste with salt and pepper. Makes 4 servings.

**10**

# Zucchini Vichy

Vichy water *is a bottled water similar to club soda.*

5 medium zucchini, shredded
1/2 cup Vichy water or club soda

1 teaspoon grated lemon peel

In a medium saucepan, combine zucchini, Vichy water or club soda and lemon peel. Cover and cook over medium heat 3 to 5 minutes or until slightly tender. Avoid overcooking. Makes 4 servings.

**20**

# Apricot-Almond Rice

*A perfect accompaniment to roast pork or chicken.*

2 tablespoons butter or margarine
1 cup uncooked long-grain white rice
1/2 cup chopped onion
1/2 cup chopped celery
1/4 teaspoon ground ginger

2 cups chicken broth or stock
3/4 cup chopped dried apricots
1/2 cup chopped dried prunes
Salt
1/2 cup sliced almonds

Melt butter or margarine in a large skillet. Add rice, onion and celery; sauté until rice is golden brown. Add ginger, broth or stock, apricots and prunes. Cover and simmer 15 minutes or until rice is tender and all liquid is absorbed. Season to taste with salt. Pour into a serving dish; garnish with almonds. Makes 4 to 6 servings.

**25**

# Rice Pilaf

*Use beef or chicken broth or stock for flavoring, depending on what Pilaf will be served with.*

2 tablespoons butter or margarine
1-1/2 cups uncooked long-grain white rice

3 cups beef or chicken broth or stock
1/4 cup sliced green onions

In a medium saucepan, melt butter or margarine. Add rice; sauté until lightly browned. Add broth or stock. Reduce heat. Cover. Cook 15 minutes or until rice is tender and all liquid is absorbed. Toss with a fork to separate rice, if needed. Pour into a serving dish; garnish with green onions. Makes 4 servings.

**25**

# Sautéed Rice

*Rice so good, you'll look for excuses to serve it.*

1 tablespoon olive oil
1 cup chopped onion
3/4 cup uncooked long-grain white rice
1/3 cup dry white wine
1-1/3 cups hot water

1/4 teaspoon salt
1 bay leaf
1/2 cup dairy sour cream
1/4 cup grated Parmesan cheese (3/4 oz.)

In a large saucepan, heat oil. Add onion; sauté slightly. Add rice; stir until rice starts to brown. Add wine, water, salt and bay leaf. Cover; simmer 15 minutes or until rice is tender and all liquid is absorbed. Remove bay leaf; stir in sour cream and cheese. Makes 4 servings.

**25**

# Polka-Dot Rice

*You can't beat this for a quick tasty dish.*

3 cups chicken broth or stock
1-1/2 cups uncooked long-grain white rice

1 (10-oz.) pkg. frozen green peas
2 tablespoons butter or margarine

In a medium saucepan, bring broth or stock to a boil; add rice. Simmer 15 minutes or until rice is tender and all liquid is absorbed. Stir in peas and butter or margarine. Makes 6 servings.

# Chili-Cheese Tomatoes

*These add color and a tangy taste to any meal.*

4 medium, firm-ripe tomatoes
1 cup dairy sour cream
1/2 teaspoon salt
1/4 teaspoon pepper
1 teaspoon sugar
1 tablespoon all-purpose flour

2 tablespoons chopped green onion
1 to 2 tablespoons canned diced
  green chilies
1 cup shredded Longhorn or
  Cheddar cheese (4 oz.)

Preheat broiler. Cut each tomato in half. Gently squeeze tomato halves to remove seeds. Arrange tomato halves, cut-sides up, on a broiler pan. In a small bowl, combine sour cream, salt, pepper, sugar, flour, green onion and green chilies; stir until well blended. Spoon sour-cream mixture over tomatoes. Sprinkle cheese evenly over sour-cream mixture. Broil, 4 inches from heat, until cheese is bubbly and golden brown, about 4 minutes. Tomatoes will be slightly warm. Makes 8 servings.

# Sautéed Cherry Tomatoes

*For a splash of color in a meal, serve these tomatoes.*

1 pint cherry tomatoes
1/4 cup butter or margarine

1 tablespoon chopped fresh basil or
1 teaspoon dried leaf basil, crumbled

Wash tomatoes; remove stems. In a large skillet, melt butter or margarine. Add basil and tomatoes. Cook over medium heat, stirring frequently, 5 minutes or until tomatoes are cooked but still hold their shape. Makes 4 to 5 servings.

# Turnips & Onions

*Turnips have an interesting flavor—try them and you'll be pleasantly surprised.*

4 medium turnips, peeled
1 medium onion, thinly sliced
1/2 cup water

3 tablespoons butter or margarine
Salt and pepper

Cut turnips in 1/4-inch wedges. Place turnip wedges, onion and water in a medium saucepan. Cover and simmer 10 minutes or until turnips are tender. Drain off water; stir in butter or margarine. Season to taste with salt and pepper. Makes 4 servings.

*A squeeze of fresh lemon juice perks up canned fruits and vegetables.*

# How to Make Lemon-Potato Wedges

1/Cut each potato in half lengthwise; then cut each half into 4 wedges.

2/Serve seasoned baked-potato wedges on a platter with sour cream as a dipping sauce.

**25**

## Lemon-Potato Wedges

*Great for appetizers, too.*

1/2 teaspoon dill weed
1 teaspoon finely grated lemon peel
3 teaspoons fresh lemon juice
1/4 cup butter or margarine, melted

3 medium baking potatoes
1/4 cup grated Parmesan cheese (3/4 oz.)
Dairy sour cream

Preheat oven to 425F (220C). In a small bowl, combine dill weed, lemon peel, lemon juice and butter or margarine. Cut each potato in half lengthwise; then each half into 4 long wedges. Place potato wedges on a baking sheet; brush with dill mixture. Sprinkle cheese over wedges. Bake 20 minutes or until potatoes are tender. Serve with sour cream as a dipping sauce. Makes 4 to 6 servings.

**10**

## Scalloped Mashed Potatoes

*Instant mashed potatoes work well because they are quick to prepare.*

1-1/4 cups instant mashed-potato flakes
1-1/4 cups chicken broth or stock
1 cup dairy sour cream

1 cup shredded Cheddar cheese (4 oz.)
1/4 cup sliced green onions

Prepare instant mashed potatoes according to package directions, using broth or stock in place of water. When potatoes are firm, stir in sour cream, cheese and green onions. Reheat over low, if needed, to desired serving temperature. Makes 5 servings.

# *Homemade Tomato Sauce*

*Delightful over hot fresh pasta.*

3/4 cup olive oil
2 garlic cloves, crushed
2 (29-oz.) cans tomatoes
1-1/2 teaspoons chopped fresh oregano or
   1/2 teaspoon dried leaf oregano

1-1/2 teaspoons chopped fresh basil or
   1/2 teaspoon dried leaf basil
1 tablespoon sugar
1/4 teaspoon salt
1/8 teaspoon pepper

Heat oil in a large saucepan. Add garlic; sauté briefly. Add tomatoes, oregano, basil, sugar, salt and pepper. Stir to break up tomatoes. Simmer over medium-low heat 20 minutes. Makes 4 to 5 cups or enough for 6 pasta servings.

### Variation

For a meat sauce, sauté 1 pound ground beef with garlic. When beef is no longer pink, drain well. Add olive oil. Proceed as above. Makes about 6 cups or enough for 8 pasta servings.

# *Quick Tomato-Corn Relish*

*Try this relish on hamburgers.*

1 (16-oz.) can stewed tomatoes,
   drained, chopped
1 (10-oz.) pkg. frozen whole-kernel corn,
   thawed

1/2 green bell pepper, chopped
1 tablespoon chopped fresh basil or
   1 teaspoon dried leaf basil
1/2 cup spicy Italian salad dressing

In a medium bowl, combine tomatoes, corn, green pepper, basil and salad dressing. Refrigerate until ready to serve. Makes 3 cups.

# *Basic Pesto Sauce*

*Fresh basil is a must in this sauce. Look for it in your supermarket's produce section.*

3 tablespoons pine nuts
2 garlic cloves
2 cups fresh basil leaves

1/3 cup grated Parmesan cheese (1 oz.)
1 cup olive oil

In a blender or food processor, finely chop nuts and garlic. Add basil, cheese and oil. Process until smooth. Makes 2-1/2 cups or enough for 6 pasta servings.

## **Tip**

*When preparing baked potatoes, boil potatoes 5 minutes, then bake as usual. Boiling reduces the baking time by about 1/2.*

# Breads

Bread in 30 minutes? Sounds impossible until you look through this chapter. There are many types of bread you can bake quickly. Breads leavened with baking powder, soda or eggs rise and bake quick enough to fit into a 30-minute meal. Yummy, aromatic breads, hot from the oven are easy and there's nothing so enticing!

There are several steps that can save you time when making breads. When making biscuits, place dough on a baking sheet. Shape dough into a square. Cut into squares with a knife. For muffins, grease tins well or use paper baking cups to line tins. They save time, and clean-up is minimal. Fill tins only 1/2 to 2/3 full. This speeds up baking time and prevents overflows. Purchase several mini-loaf pans. Bread will bake faster and it eliminates slicing. Serving each person his own loaf gives an elegant feel to the meal.

Be sure to preheat your oven before baking. Heat activates the rising process quickly for a lighter loaf. It also makes the baking time faster and more accurate. If you haven't checked your oven temperature recently, buy an oven thermometer to check it. Accuracy is the key to successful baking.

Breads freeze well if wrapped tightly to prevent drying. Make two or three recipes when you have time. Then freeze for future use. Bread slices best when it is slightly frozen. You get a nice thin slice with very few crumbs. To thaw bread, wrap it in foil. Place in a 350F (175C) oven 5 to 10 minutes. This will also warm the bread for best flavor. Bread slices thaw quicker than a complete loaf.

Serving a main course in a bread boat or popover lends an air of originality. You could even hollow out a large loaf and use it as a serving dish!

If you don't have time to bake your own bread, purchase it from a good bakery. Then add your own personal touches. Taco-Flavored French Bread is a great addition to a broiled or barbecued meal. Marmalade-Cream Bagels brighten up any breakfast. Freshly purchased croissants, warmed in your oven, need nothing more than sweet butter to make them irresistible.

To save time, let guests butter their bread. Serve warm bread with garlic butter and plain butter. This gives guests a choice and saves you time. When reheating bread, wrap it in foil to keep the crust soft. If you want a crisp crust, such as for croissants, place the bread on a baking sheet. Do not cover it. To keep bread warm while serving, wrap it in a napkin in an attractive basket.

Many people feel a meal is incomplete without a type of bread—biscuits, muffins, breadsticks, popovers. The list is endless. Be sure to serve fresh bread with sweet butter or something even more special, such as an herb-flavored butter or homemade jam. Offer a tasty, light bread with a salad or soup and you have a complete meal.

## Nutty Cranberry Ring

*Fresh frozen cranberries are now available year-round.*

2/3 cup milk
2 eggs
1/3 cup vegetable oil
1/2 teaspoon baking soda
2 teaspoons baking powder

2 cups all-purpose flour
1 cup sugar
1 teaspoon grated lemon peel
1-1/2 cups fresh cranberries
1/2 cup chopped walnuts

Preheat oven to 375F (190C). Grease and flour an 8-cup Bundt pan or ring mold; set aside. In a medium bowl, combine milk, eggs, oil, baking soda and baking powder. Stir in flour, sugar and lemon peel; blend well. Fold in cranberries and walnuts. Pour into greased pan. Bake 25 minutes or until a wooden pick inserted in ring comes out clean. Makes 6 to 8 servings.

## Strawberry-Rhubarb Ring

*Great for those who love rhubarb.*

1 cup packed brown sugar
1/3 cup vegetable oil
1 egg
1 teaspoon vanilla extract
2-1/2 cups all-purpose flour
1 teaspoon baking soda

1 teaspoon baking powder
1/2 teaspoon salt
1 cup thinly sliced fresh or frozen rhubarb
1 cup sliced fresh or
    unsweetened frozen strawberries

Preheat oven to 400F (205C). Grease an 8-cup Bundt pan or ring mold; set aside. In a medium bowl, combine brown sugar, oil, egg and vanilla. Stir in flour, baking soda, baking powder and salt. When dough is completely blended, lightly fold in rhubarb and strawberries. Pour into greased pan. Bake 25 minutes or until a wooden pick inserted in ring comes out clean. Makes 6 to 8 servings.

# *How to Make Orange-Marmalade Coffeecake*

1/Starting at jam edge, cut pastry on both sides into 1-1/2-inch-wide strips.

2/Alternating side to side, fold dough strips over top of marmalade, pressing lightly to seal.

**25**

## *Orange-Marmalade Coffeecake*    Photo on page 17.

*Substitute raspberry, apricot or your favorite jam for a different flavor.*

| | |
|---|---|
| **2 cups buttermilk baking mix** | **2 tablespoons milk** |
| **1/2 teaspoon ground cinnamon** | **All-purpose flour** |
| **1 (3-oz.) pkg. cream cheese,** | **1 cup orange marmalade** |
| **room temperature** | **Powdered sugar** |
| **1/4 cup butter or margarine,** | |
| **room temperature** | |

Preheat oven to 425F (220C). Grease a 15" x 10" baking sheet; set aside. In a medium bowl or food processor, combine baking mix, cinnamon, cream cheese and butter or margarine until crumbly. Blend in milk. Dough will be slightly stiff. Turn out dough on a lightly floured board; knead 10 times. Place on greased baking sheet. Roll out dough to a 14" x 9" rectangle. Spread 3/4 cup marmalade lengthwise down center 1/3 of dough. Starting at jam edge, cut pastry on both sides into 1-1/2-inch-wide strips, cutting outward. Alternating sides, fold dough strips over top of marmalade. Pinch ends together to prevent filling leaking. Bake 15 minutes or until golden brown. Dust with powdered sugar. Garnish with remaining 1/4 cup marmalade. Makes 6 servings.

# Square Biscuits

*Serve this scone-type bread hot with butter and jam.*

**2 cups buttermilk baking mix**          **2/3 cup milk**
**1/2 teaspoon baking soda**

Preheat oven to 450F (230C). In a medium bowl, combine all ingredients to make a soft dough. Turn out dough on a lightly floured surface; knead 15 times. Place on an ungreased baking sheet. Pat into an 8-inch square. Cut into 2-inch squares. Do not separate dough pieces. Bake 10 to 15 minutes. Makes 16 biscuits.

# Herb-Cheese-Topped Bagels

*A perfect appetizer or accompaniment to steaming soup.*

**3 bagels, split**                          **1/8 teaspoon dried leaf marjoram, crumbled**
**1 (3-oz.) pkg. whipped cream cheese**      **1/8 teaspoon dried leaf basil, crumbled**
**1/8 teaspoon caraway seeds**

Toast bagel halves. In a small bowl, combine cream cheese, caraway seeds, marjoram and basil. Spread on toasted bagels. Makes 6 servings.

# Marmalade-Cream Bagels

*Serve for breakfast or with a fruit salad at lunch.*

**2 bagels, split**                          **2 tablespoons orange marmalade**
**1 (3-oz.) pkg. whipped cream cheese**

Toast bagel halves. In a small bowl, combine cream cheese and marmalade. Spread on toasted bagels. Makes 4 servings.

**25**

# Molasses-Orange-Bran Muffins

*These muffins freeze well and defrost quickly.*

2-1/2 cups all-purpose flour
2 teaspoons baking powder
1/2 teaspoon baking soda
1 teaspoon salt
1-1/2 cups whole-bran cereal

1 egg, beaten
1 cup molasses
3/4 cup orange juice
1 tablespoon grated orange peel
1 cup raisins

Preheat oven to 400F (205C). Grease 18 muffin cups or line with paper liners; set aside. In a large bowl, combine flour, baking powder, baking soda, salt and cereal. Stir in egg, molasses, orange juice, orange peel and raisins until dry ingredients are moistened. Spoon batter evenly into prepared muffin cups. Bake 20 minutes or until browned. Immediately remove from pan. Serve warm. Makes 18 muffins.

**25**

# Apple-Bran Muffins

*Using paper liners for muffin cups makes preparation and clean-up easier.*

1/2 cup whole-bran cereal
1-1/2 cups all-purpose flour
1/2 cup sugar
1/2 teaspoon ground cinnamon
1/4 teaspoon ground nutmeg
4 teaspoons baking powder

1/2 teaspoon salt
1 cup milk
1 egg
1/4 cup butter or margarine, melted
3/4 cup finely chopped apple

Preheat oven to 425F (220C). Grease 12 muffin cups or line with paper liners; set aside. In a medium bowl, combine cereal, flour, sugar, cinnamon, nutmeg, baking powder and salt. Stir in milk, egg and butter or margarine until dry ingredients are moistened. Fold in apple. Spoon batter evenly into prepared muffin cups. Bake 20 minutes or until browned. Immediately remove from pan. Serve warm. Makes 12 muffins.

**25**

# Bacon-Cheese Muffins

*Serve warm for a soft cheesy center.*

1-1/2 cups buttermilk baking mix
1/2 cup milk
1/3 cup butter or margarine, melted
1 egg
12 crisp-cooked bacon slices, crumbled

1/3 cup shredded zucchini
1/3 cup chopped onion
2 oz. Cheddar cheese,
    cut in 12 (1/2-inch) cubes

Preheat oven to 425F (220C). Grease 12 muffin cups or line with paper liners; set aside. In a medium bowl, combine baking mix, milk, butter or margarine and egg; stir lightly to combine. Stir in bacon, zucchini and onion. Spoon batter evenly into prepared muffin cups. Press a cheese cube in center of each muffin. Bake 15 to 20 minutes or until golden brown. Immediately remove from pan. Serve while warm. Makes 12 muffins.

Muffins clockwise: Whole-Wheat-Date Muffins, page 126; Molasses-Orange-Bran Muffins, above; and Cherry-Almond Muffins, page 126. Spreads, top to bottom: Amaretto-Cream-Cheese Spread, page 131; Lemon-Honey Butter, page 131; and Pecan Butter, page 131.

# Whole-Wheat-Blueberry Muffins

*Healthy and tasty, too.*

1 cup all-purpose flour
3/4 cup whole-wheat flour
1/2 teaspoon salt
1/4 teaspoon baking soda
2 teaspoons baking powder
1/2 teaspoon ground cinnamon

3/4 cup milk
1 egg, beaten
1/2 cup butter or margarine, melted
1/2 cup molasses
1 cup fresh or frozen blueberries

Preheat oven to 375F (190C). Grease 12 muffin cups or line with paper liners; set aside. In a medium bowl, combine all-purpose flour, whole-wheat flour, salt, baking soda, baking powder and cinnamon. Stir in milk, egg, butter or margarine and molasses until dry ingredients are moistened. Gently fold in blueberries. Spoon batter evenly into prepared muffin cups. Bake 20 minutes or until browned. Immediately remove from pan. Serve warm. Makes 12 muffins.

# Whole-Wheat-Date Muffins    *Photo on page 125.*

*A good dinner muffin that isn't too sweet.*

1 cup whole-wheat flour
1 cup yellow cornmeal
3-1/2 teaspoons baking powder
2 tablespoons sugar
1 teaspoon salt

3/4 cup chopped dates
1 egg, slightly beaten
1 cup milk
1/4 cup butter or margarine, melted

Preheat oven to 425F (220C). Grease 12 muffin cups or line with paper liners; set aside. In a medium bowl, combine whole-wheat flour, cornmeal, baking powder, sugar, salt and dates. In a small bowl, beat together egg, milk and butter or margarine; stir into dry ingredients until dry ingredients are moistened. Spoon batter evenly into prepared muffin cups. Bake 20 minutes or until browned. Immediately remove from pan. Serve warm. Makes 12 muffins.

# Cherry-Almond Muffins    *Photo on page 125.*

*Fresh hot bread for breakfast is the ideal way to start a day.*

1/2 cup milk
1 egg
1/4 cup butter or margarine, melted
1 teaspoon almond extract
1-1/2 cups all-purpose flour
1-1/2 teaspoons baking powder

1/2 teaspoon salt
1/3 cup sugar
1/2 cup chopped almonds
1 (16-oz.) can pitted red tart cherries,
   drained

Preheat oven to 425F (220C). Grease 12 muffin cups or line with paper liners; set aside. In a medium bowl, combine milk, egg, butter or margarine and almond extract. Stir in flour, baking powder, salt, sugar and almonds; blend well. Gently fold in drained cherries. Spoon batter evenly into prepared muffin cups. Bake 20 minutes or until golden brown. Immediately remove from pan. Serve warm. Makes 12 muffins.

# *How to Make Raisin-Oatmeal Scones*

1/Cut each dough circle into 6 wedges.

2/Serve scones with a hot beverage and favorite spread.

**25**

## *Raisin-Oatmeal Scones*

*Soaking raisins in hot water keeps them moist throughout baking.*

| | |
|---|---|
| 1/2 cup raisins | 2 cups regular or |
| 1 cup boiling water | quick-cooking rolled oats |
| 2 cups all-purpose flour | 1/4 cup chilled butter or margarine |
| 1/4 cup sugar | 2 eggs |
| 1 tablespoon baking powder | 1/3 cup milk or half and half |

Preheat oven to 400F (205C). Grease a large baking sheet. In a small bowl, combine raisins and boiling water; set aside. In a medium bowl or food processor, combine flour, sugar, baking powder and oats. Cut in butter or margarine until mixture is crumbly. Blend in eggs and milk or half and half. Drain raisins; stir into dough. Turn out dough on a lightly floured board; knead 10 times. Divide dough into thirds. Place on greased baking sheet; pat each third into a circle about 3/4-inch thick. Cut each circle in 6 wedges. Bake 15 to 20 minutes. Separate wedges; cool on a wire rack. Makes 18 scones.

**30**

# Miniature Sherry Loaves

*A lovely tea bread, great for a luncheon or afternoon tea.*

3 cups all-purpose flour
1 cup sugar
4 teaspoons baking powder
1 teaspoon salt
2 teaspoons grated lemon peel

1 cup chopped pecans
1 cup milk
1/3 cup butter or margarine, melted
1 egg, beaten
1/2 cup dry sherry

Preheat oven to 400F (205C). Grease 4 (5" x 3") loaf pans; set aside. In a medium bowl, combine flour, sugar, baking powder, salt, lemon peel and 3/4 cup pecans. All at once, add milk, butter or margarine, egg and sherry; stir vigorously to blend. Divide batter evenly between greased pans. Sprinkle remaining pecans over top. Bake 20 to 25 minutes or until a wooden pick inserted in center comes out clean. Makes 4 loaves.

**28**

# Miniature Gougères

*Gougères are usually made in a ring large enough to serve six to eight people.*

1/2 cup water
1/4 cup butter or margarine
1/2 cup all-purpose flour
1 teaspoon Dijon-style mustard

2 eggs
1/2 cup shredded Swiss cheese (2 oz.)
1/4 cup thinly sliced green onions

Preheat oven to 400F (205C). Grease a large baking sheet; set aside. In a medium saucepan, bring water and butter or margarine to a boil. Remove from heat. Add flour and mustard, stirring until mixture gathers in a ball. Add eggs, 1 at a time, completely stirring in each. Stir in cheese and green onions. Drop batter onto greased baking sheet making 12 even mounds. Bake 20 minutes or until golden brown and dry in appearance. Makes 12 servings.

**8**

# Parmesan Pumpernickel

*This thinly sliced bread is often served with salads in fine restaurants.*

3 tablespoons butter or margarine
8 thin slices pumpernickel bread

1 tablespoon freshly grated Parmesan cheese

Preheat broiler. Spread butter or margarine on bread all the way out to the edges. Sprinkle cheese over buttered bread. Place on a baking sheet. Broil, 4 inches from heat, 1 to 2 minutes or until hot and crisp. Makes 4 servings.

**25**

# Chili-Custard Corn Bread

*Corn bread good enough to make a whole meal.*

| | |
|---|---|
| 1 cup all-purpose flour | 1 cup milk |
| 1 cup yellow cornmeal | 2 eggs, beaten |
| 3 tablespoons sugar | 1 cup dairy sour cream |
| 5 teaspoons baking powder | 1 tablespoon all-purpose flour |
| 1/2 teaspoon salt | 1 egg, slightly beaten |
| 1/4 cup melted butter | 1 (4-oz.) can diced green chilies |

Preheat oven to 400F (205C). Grease an 8-inch-square baking pan; set aside. In a large bowl, combine 1 cup flour, cornmeal, sugar, baking powder and salt. Pour in butter, milk and 2 eggs; blend well. Pour mixture into greased pan. Bake 15 minutes. Meanwhile, in a small bowl, combine sour cream, 1 tablespoon flour, 1 egg and chilies. Remove corn bread from oven; spread sour-cream mixture over hot bread. Return to oven; bake 5 to 8 minutes longer. Cut in 2-inch squares. Serve hot. Makes 16 pieces.

**30**

# Cheddar-Corn Bread

*This bread is made with corn instead of cornmeal.*

| | |
|---|---|
| 1/4 cup butter or margarine | 1 egg, beaten |
| 2 medium onions, chopped | 1/2 cup milk |
| 1 cup dairy sour cream | 1 (8-1/2-oz.) can cream-style corn |
| 1 cup shredded Cheddar cheese (4 oz.) | 3 drops hot-pepper sauce |
| 1-1/2 cups buttermilk baking mix | |

Preheat oven to 450F (230C). Grease an 8-inch-square baking pan; set aside. In a medium skillet, melt butter or margarine. Add onions; sauté over high heat until transparent. Remove from heat. Stir in sour cream and 1/2 cup cheese; set aside. In a medium bowl, combine baking mix, egg, milk, corn and hot-pepper sauce. Spread dough in greased pan. Gently spoon onion mixture over dough. Top with remaining 1/2 cup cheese. Bake 25 minutes or until done. Cut into squares. Serve warm. Makes 6 to 9 servings.

# Tip

*If a recipe calls for buttermilk or sour milk and you have neither, add 1 tablespoon vinegar or lemon juice to 1 cup fresh milk; let stand 5 minutes.*

# How to Make Poppy-Sesame Breadsticks

1/Cut each split bun lengthwise into 3 strips; separate each into 6 strips.

2/Dip bread strips in butter; roll in seed mixture. Place on a baking sheet.

**20**

## Poppy-Sesame Breadsticks

*A great way to use leftover hot-dog buns.*

**2 split hot-dog buns**
**1/2 cup butter, melted**

**1 tablespoon sesame seeds**
**1 tablespoon poppy seeds**

Preheat oven to 350F (175C). Cut each bun half lengthwise into 3 strips, making a total of 12 strips. Pour melted butter in a pie plate. In another pie plate, combine seeds. Dip each bread strip in butter; then roll in seed mixture. Place on an ungreased baking sheet. Bake 15 minutes or until crisp. Makes 12 breadsticks.

# Bread Toppings for that Homemade Taste

Be sure to purchase fresh, top-quality bread for these recipes. Homemade toppings make them special.

**Cheesy French Bread**
1 French-bread loaf
1/2 cup butter or margarine, room temperature
1/4 cup grated Parmesan cheese (3/4 oz.)

Preheat oven to 350F (175C). Cut bread in half lengthwise. Spread both halves with butter or margarine; sprinkle both halves with cheese. Wrap foil around sides and bottom of each half, leaving top open. Bake 10 minutes or until warm through. Cut or tear into serving pieces. Makes 6 to 8 servings.

**Savory Bagels**
3 bagels, cut in half
1/4 cup butter or margarine, room temperature
2 tablespoons chopped green onion
1/2 cup shredded sharp Cheddar cheese (2 oz.)
1/2 teaspoon poppy seeds

Preheat broiler. Spread bagel halves with butter or margarine; arrange on a baking sheet. In a small bowl, combine green onion, cheese and poppy seeds. Sprinkle buttered side of bagels with onion mixture. Broil, 6 inches from heat, until cheese melts and is bubbly. Makes 6 servings.

**Seed-Topped Rolls**
12 unbaked Brown & Serve rolls
3 tablespoons butter, melted
1 tablespoon sesame seeds or poppy seeds

Preheat oven to 350F (175C). Place rolls on a baking sheet. Brush butter over roll tops; sprinkle with sesame seeds or poppy seeds. Bake 10 to 15 minutes or until golden brown. Makes 12 rolls.

**Taco-Flavored French Bread**
1 French-bread loaf
1/2 cup butter or margarine, room temperature
1 cup shredded taco-flavor chili cheese (4 oz.)

Preheat oven to 350F (175C). Cut bread in half lengthwise. Spread both halves with butter or margarine; sprinkle both halves with cheese. Wrap foil around sides and bottom of each half, leaving top open. Bake 10 to 15 minutes or until cheese is melted and bread is warm through. Cut or tear into serving pieces. Makes 6 to 8 servings.

# Flavored Butters & Spreads

Use the following combinations or create your own favorite flavored butter or spread. To prepare each, in a blender, food processor or small bowl, combine all ingredients until smooth and fluffy.

**Pecan Butter**
*Photo on page 125.*
1/2 cup butter or margarine, room temperature
2 tablespoons brown sugar
2 tablespoons finely chopped pecans

**Lemon-Honey Butter**
*Photo on page 125.*
1/2 cup butter or margarine, room temperature
1/2 cup honey
1/2 teaspoon finely grated lemon peel

**Amaretto-Cream-Cheese Spread**
*Photo on page 125.*
1 (3-oz.) pkg. cream cheese, room temperature
1 tablespoon amaretto liqueur

**Pineapple-Cheese Spread**
1 (3-oz.) pkg. cream cheese, room temperature
2 tablespoons drained crushed pineapple

**Honey Butter**
Prepare Lemon-Honey Butter, omitting lemon peel.

# Desserts

Desserts are basically divided into two groups: classics and favorites. Many belong to both categories. Unfortunately, both are usually expected to take considerable preparation. A look through these recipes will surprise you at how many delicious treats can be prepared in only a few minutes. You will also find suggestions for desserts you might not have thought of before.

Plan dessert according to the flavors and richness of the meal. Also consider your overall time schedule; the amount of refrigerator, freezer or oven space you have available; and the time needed to chill, freeze or cook the food.

There are many ways to save preparation time with desserts. Chocolate-Mint-Frosted Brownies are frosted by setting chocolate-covered mint candies on the hot brownies as they come from the oven. About five minutes later, when the candies have softened, swirl the chocolate over the brownies as a frosting. Some cakes are so tasty they don't need a frosting. One of my favorite quick-to-fix-but-elegant desserts is Blueberries & Grand Marnier Whipped Cream. For a five-minute dessert, you can't get much nicer.

When entertaining in the afternoon or following dinner, try serving a dessert buffet. Your guests will be amazed. Cut serving pieces small so guests can taste each one. Plan one type of dessert for every four people. Send extras home with guests or wrap them tightly to freeze for future use. When serving leftovers, be sure to dish them up in the kitchen. Guests will never know the dessert wasn't made especially for them.

Cookies are a quick-to-make item if you can bake them all at once. These cookie recipes are designed for just that. Bar cookies can be baked in one pan, then cut for serving.

You can often prepare parts of a dessert ahead of time, such as pie crust. Roll out pastry and place in a pie pan; securely wrap with foil. Freeze until ready to use. There is no need to defrost a frozen unbaked pie shell. Bake shell, then cool and fill with a no-bake filling, such as Banana-Sour-Cream Pudding. You will have a fast pie for dessert. Unbaked pie shells can also be filled and then baked.

When reading a recipe, be sure to check the full preparation time. Some items need a long baking or chilling time.

Freshness and lightness are desirable traits in desserts, especially after a filling meal. Strawberry Grand Marnier Ice Cream is fabulous and it's easy to prepare using a food processor or blender. It can be freezing while you serve the meal. Then at the last minute, whip and serve the ice cream. Substitute raspberries or peaches for a different taste.

Serving dishes need consideration. How the dessert will look is always important. When you are working on a limited time schedule, the size of the serving dish can speed up baking or cooling time. Many items you may think impossible for a 30-minute schedule can be done with a little re-arrangement of pan size.

Garnishing desserts can really be fun, but don't get carried away. Simple-but-elegant is the best way. A pretty idea for Lemon-Puff Soufflé is a thin strip of lemon peel, tied in a knot. Place it on top of the soufflé.

Another simple dessert is a plate of Rapid Rocky-Road Fudge served with coffee or tea. Guests can help themselves. Desserts of this type look like a lot more work than they really are. Who can resist good chocolate?

Luscious desserts are not always time consuming and calorie laden! These recipes are simple to prepare, wonderful to look at and taste outstanding. What are you waiting for? ☙

---

**25**

# *Sautéed Apples with Custard Sauce*

*An excellent fall or winter dessert when apples are plentiful.*

| | |
|---|---|
| **4 large red cooking apples, cored** | **1/2 cup golden raisins** |
| **3 tablespoons butter or margarine** | **Custard Sauce, see below** |
| **1/2 teaspoon ground cinnamon** | |

**Custard Sauce**

| | |
|---|---|
| **1/3 cup sugar** | **2 egg yolks, slightly beaten** |
| **2 tablespoons cornstarch** | **2 tablespoons butter** |
| **1/8 teaspoon salt** | **1/4 cup brandy or rum** |
| **1-3/4 cups milk** | |

Cut apples into 1/2-inch wedges, making about 5 cups. Melt butter or margarine in a 10-inch skillet. Add apple wedges. Sprinkle cinnamon over apple wedges. Sauté over medium-low heat 5 minutes, stirring carefully. Sprinkle with raisins. Reduce heat to lowest setting. Cover and cook 12 minutes or until tender. Prepare Custard Sauce. Serve warm over sautéed apples. Makes 6 servings.

**Custard Sauce:**
In a medium saucepan, combine sugar, cornstarch and salt. Gradually stir in milk. Cook over medium-low heat, stirring constantly, until mixture thickens. Remove from heat. Stir a small amount of mixture into egg yolks. Return saucepan to heat. Stir egg mixture into mixture in saucepan. Cook, stirring constantly, until mixture simmers and thickens slightly. Remove from heat. Stir in butter and brandy or rum until butter melts.

---

# Tip

*Three medium peaches equal 1 pound or 3 cups sliced peaches, or 2 cups peach puree. About 1-1/4 pounds fresh peaches equal 1 pint frozen or canned peaches.*

**28**

# Plum Crispy

*For a midwinter treat, replace plums with peeled apples.*

| | |
|---|---|
| **4 cups fresh plum slices** | **1 egg, beaten** |
| **3/4 cup sugar** | **1/2 teaspoon baking soda** |
| **1/4 teaspoon ground cinnamon** | **1 teaspoon vanilla extract** |
| **1 tablespoon butter or margarine** | **1/2 cup all-purpose flour** |

Preheat oven to 400F (205C). Grease an 8-inch-square baking pan. Place plum slices in greased pan. In a small bowl, combine 1/4 cup sugar and cinnamon; sprinkle over plums. In a medium bowl, cream together butter or margarine and 1/2 cup sugar. Stir in egg, baking soda, vanilla and flour. Spread batter evenly over plums. Bake 20 minutes or until top is golden brown. Makes 6 to 8 servings.

**30**

# Pecan Bread-Pudding

*Serve warm and fresh from the oven.*

| | |
|---|---|
| **1-1/2 cups half and half** | **1/4 teaspoon ground nutmeg** |
| **1/3 cup chopped pecans** | **1/4 teaspoon salt** |
| **2 eggs, slightly beaten** | **6 to 8 stale raisin-bread slices,** |
| **1/3 cup sugar** | **cut in 1-inch cubes** |
| **1/2 teaspoon vanilla extract** | **Custard Sauce, page 133** |
| **1/2 teaspoon ground cinnamon** | |

Preheat oven to 375F (190C). Butter a 1-quart ring mold; set aside. In a medium bowl, beat together half and half, pecans, eggs, sugar, vanilla, cinnamon, nutmeg and salt. Stir in bread cubes until bread absorbs most of liquid. Pour into buttered mold. Place mold in a 2-quart casserole. Fill outer dish with boiling water to within 1 inch of the top of the mold. Bake 20 minutes or until golden brown and set. While baking, prepare Custard Sauce. Unmold pudding. Serve warm sauce spooned over individual servings. Makes 4 to 6 servings.

**27**

# Peach-Macaroon Melba    *Photo on pages 78 and 79.*

*To make this an authentic melba, top with vanilla ice cream.*

| | |
|---|---|
| **1/3 cup raspberry jelly** | **8 crisp macaroons** |
| **1/4 cup water** | **2 tablespoons butter or margarine** |
| **6 fresh peaches, peeled** | **Whipping cream or half and half** |

Preheat oven to 400F (205C). In a small saucepan, bring jelly and water to a boil; boil 3 minutes. Cut each peach into 8 wedges; arrange in a single layer in a 13'' x 9'' baking dish. Pour hot jelly mixture over peaches. Crush macaroons with a rolling pin or in a food processor; sprinkle over peaches. Dot peaches with butter or margarine. Bake 20 minutes or until peaches are tender. Serve hot or cold with cream. Makes 4 to 6 servings.

*If only raspberry jam can be found, strain after cooking to remove seeds.*

# *Mincemeat Cobbler*

**22**

*Try mincemeat at other times of the year, not just Christmas.*

**1 (16-oz.) jar mincemeat**
**1 apple, peeled, finely chopped**
**1/4 cup brandy**
**1/2 cup walnuts**
**1 cup fresh cranberries, if desired**

**1 cup all-purpose flour**
**1/4 cup butter or margarine**
**2 tablespoons sugar**
**1/2 teaspoon salt**
**3 to 4 tablespoons cold water**

Preheat oven to 400F (205C). Grease a 10-inch oval baking dish; set aside. In a medium saucepan, combine mincemeat, apple, brandy, walnuts and cranberries, if desired. Simmer over medium heat 5 minutes. In a medium bowl or food processor, combine flour, butter or margarine, sugar and salt. Work mixture until crumbly; then blend in enough water to form a workable dough. Roll out dough on waxed paper to an 8-inch oval. Using your fingers, flute edge all the way around. Pour hot mincemeat mixture into greased dish. Top with fluted pastry. Bake 10 minutes or until crust is lightly browned. Makes 6 to 8 servings.

**Variation**

Use 2 apples if cranberries are not used.

# *Bananas Flambé*

**12**

*A superb way to end a lovely meal.*

**2 tablespoons butter or margarine**
**1 (6-oz.) can frozen-orange-juice concentrate,**
  **thawed**
**1/2 cup packed brown sugar**
**1/4 cup Grand Marnier or**
  **other orange liqueur**

**3 medium bananas, cut in**
  **1/2-inch diagonal slices**
**1/4 cup brandy**
**1 qt. or more, rich vanilla ice cream**

In a 10-inch skillet over medium heat, heat butter or margarine, orange-juice concentrate, brown sugar and liqueur. Stir to blend. Add bananas; stir, turning bananas to coat with sauce. Cook 5 minutes or until bananas are hot. Warm brandy in a small saucepan over low heat until bubbles begin to appear around edge of pan. Pour warm brandy over bananas. Using a long match, carefully ignite brandy. Shake gently until flame goes out. Prepare 6 dessert dishes of vanilla ice cream. Spoon bananas and sauce evenly over ice cream. Makes 6 servings.

**Tip**

*Cupcakes take approximately 1/3 the baking time as a layer cake.*

# How to Make Chocolate-Orange Torte

1/Layer cake slices, alternating with marmalade and frosting.

2/Frost entire cake. Refrigerate until ready to slice and serve.

**8**

# Chocolate-Orange Torte

*Your guests never need to know how simple this masterpiece is to make.*

**1 (10-3/4-oz.) loaf-shape pound cake**
**2/3 cup orange marmalade**

**1 (16.5-oz.) can ready-to-spread**
**chocolate frosting**

Using a very sharp knife, cut cake into 4 thin lengthwise layers. Place bottom cake layer on a platter. Spread with 1/3 cup marmalade. Place another cake layer on top; spread with 1/3 cup frosting. Place next layer on top; spread with remaining marmalade. Place final layer on top. Frost top and sides of cake with chocolate frosting. Refrigerate until ready to serve. Cut chilled cake into thin slices. Can be made the day before. Makes 8 servings.

## Tip

*To quickly peel tomatoes, peaches or small boiling onions, plunge them into boiling water for 30 to 60 seconds. Immediately plunge them into ice water to cool. Skins will slip off easily.*

**17**

# Quick Dobos Torte

*Use a ready-made pound cake for this quick, delicious torte.*

1 (10-3/4-oz.) loaf-shape pound cake
3 cups powdered sugar
2 eggs
1/2 cup milk
1/2 cup vegetable shortening

1 cup (6 oz.) semisweet chocolate pieces,
  melted
2 teaspoons vanilla extract
Sliced almonds

Using a very sharp knife, cut cake into 6 thin lengthwise layers. To make slicing easier, insert wooden picks in side of cake to form a cutting line. Beat together sugar, eggs, milk, shortening, chocolate and vanilla. Mixture should be thick but spreadable. Place bottom cake layer on a platter. Spread with chocolate mixture. Repeat until all layers are stacked and frosted. Frost top and sides of cake. Sprinkle almonds over top of cake. Refrigerate until ready to serve. Cut chilled cake into thin slices. Makes 8 servings.

**15**

# Rum-Raisin Trifle

*If planning ahead, soak raisins and almonds in rum overnight for a rich flavor.*

1/2 cup light rum
3/4 cup golden raisins
1/2 cup chopped almonds
1 cup whipping cream

1 (3-oz.) pkg. instant vanilla-pudding mix
2-1/2 cups milk
1 loaf-shape angel food cake,
  cut into 1/2-inch cubes

In a small bowl, combine rum, raisins and almonds; set aside. In another bowl, whip cream until stiff; set aside. In a medium bowl, combine pudding mix and milk, stirring until thickened. Fold in 1/2 of the whipped cream. In a large glass bowl, layer 1/3 of the cake cubes, almond mixture and pudding. Repeat layering twice. Top with remaining whipped cream. Cover with plastic wrap. Chill in freezer until ready to serve. If longer than 1 hour, chill in refrigerator. Makes 8 servings.

**30**

# Glazed Nectarines

*Peaches work well in place of nectarines, but they must be peeled.*

4 large nectarines
1/4 cup dry sherry or orange juice
2 tablespoons sugar

1/2 cup orange marmalade
1 tablespoon fresh lemon juice
Vanilla ice cream

Preheat oven to 375F (190C). Quarter and remove pits from nectarines. Arrange fruit in a shallow 13" x 9" baking dish. In a small bowl, combine sherry or orange juice, sugar, marmalade and lemon juice; pour over nectarines. Cover with foil. Bake 20 to 25 minutes. Remove cover and cool slightly. Scoop ice cream into 4 dessert dishes. Top with nectarines and glaze. Makes 4 servings.

**30**

# Apricot Tart

*An idea from a French cafeteria where the pastries were beautiful.*

| | |
|---|---|
| 1 cup all-purpose flour | 3 tablespoons water |
| 1/4 cup butter or margarine | 1/4 cup sugar |
| 1/4 teaspoon salt | 1 (29-oz.) can apricot halves, drained |

Preheat oven to 450F (230C). In a medium bowl, combine flour, butter or margarine and salt; blend until crumbly. Stir in water until dough forms a ball. On a baking sheet, pat dough into a 9-inch circle. Using your fingers, flute edge to a 1/2-inch height. Sprinkle 3 tablespoons sugar over dough. Arrange apricots on dough, cut-side down, in a circular pattern to cover dough completely. Cut a few apricots into quarters to fill in any holes between apricot halves. Bake 20 minutes. Remove from oven; immediately sprinkle remaining 1 tablespoon sugar over hot apricots. Makes 8 servings.

**30**

# Caramel-Pecan Tart

*Tart pastry, unlike pie pastry, cannot be overworked.*

| | |
|---|---|
| 1 cup all-purpose flour | 3/4 cup whipping cream |
| 1/2 cup butter or margarine | 2/3 cup packed brown sugar |
| 1/2 teaspoon almond extract | 1-1/2 cups chopped pecans |
| 2 tablespoons milk | 1 teaspoon orange flavoring |

Preheat oven to 425F (220C). In a medium bowl or food processor, combine flour, butter or margarine, almond extract and milk; blend until combined. Using your hands, press dough into bottom and side of a 10-inch tart pan with removable bottom, if possible. Bake 5 minutes. Meanwhile, in a small saucepan. combine whipping cream and brown sugar over medium heat. Bring to a boil; boil 1 minute. Add pecans and orange flavoring. Cook 2 minutes longer, stirring constantly, to warm pecans. Pour into partially baked tart shell. Bake 20 minutes or until top of tart is set. Makes 12 servings.

**27**

# 1-2-3 Scottish Shortbread

*Rice flour may be substituted for half the all-purpose flour for an extra-crisp cookie.*

| | |
|---|---|
| 1/2 cup sugar | 2 cups all-purpose flour |
| 1 cup butter | 1/2 teaspoon vanilla extract |

Preheat oven to 350F (175C). In a medium bowl, cream together sugar and butter. Blend in flour and vanilla. Using your fingers, pat dough into a 10-inch square on an ungreased baking sheet. Dough should be about 1/2 inch thick. Prick dough with a fork. Cut into 16 (2-1/2-inch) squares but do not pull apart. Bake 15 to 20 minutes or until light golden. Cool slightly; then gently break into squares. Makes 16 servings.

**25**

# Lemon-Puff Soufflé

*A lemon sauce on the bottom is a tasty topping when this dish is served.*

1/2 cup butter or margarine
1-1/4 cups granulated sugar
1 tablespoon cornstarch
1/3 cup fresh lemon juice
1 teaspoon grated lemon peel

4 eggs, separated
1/2 teaspoon cream of tartar
2 tablespoons all-purpose flour
Powdered sugar

Preheat oven to 350F (175C). In a medium saucepan, melt butter or margarine over medium heat. In a small bowl, combine 3/4 cup granulated sugar and cornstarch; stir mixture into melted butter or margarine. Add lemon juice and peel. Bring mixture to a boil, stirring constantly, until slightly thickened. Pour into a 1-1/2-quart flat baking dish. In a large bowl, beat egg whites and cream of tartar until stiff peaks form. Slowly beat in remaining 1/2 cup granulated sugar until egg whites are very stiff. In another bowl, beat together egg yolks and flour until yolks are thickened. Gently fold egg-yolk mixture into beaten egg whites. Mound egg-white mixture on top of lemon sauce, covering all the sauce. Bake 15 minutes or until whites are set. Remove from oven. Sift powdered sugar over top. To serve, spoon lemon sauce over top of meringue. Makes 4 servings.

**23**

# Soufflé Amaretto

*Substitute your favorite liqueur for amaretto. Try crème de menthe, Grand Marnier or Sambuca.*

3/4 cup milk
3 tablespoons sugar
5 eggs, separated

1/4 teaspoon cream of tartar
1/4 cup amaretto or other liqueur

Preheat oven to 450F (230C). In a medium saucepan, combine milk and sugar. Bring to a boil over medium heat; remove from heat. Beat egg yolks in a medium bowl; gradually stir warm milk mixture into beaten yolks. In a medium bowl, beat egg whites and cream of tartar until stiff. Fold egg-yolk mixture and liqueur into beaten egg whites. Pour mixture into a 2-quart soufflé dish. Bake 15 minutes. Makes 8 servings.

**20**

# Banana-Sour-Cream Pudding

*For a change, try instant chocolate or pistachio pudding in place of banana pudding.*

1-1/4 cups milk
1 (5-5/8-oz.) pkg. instant
   banana-pudding mix

1 cup dairy sour cream
2 bananas

In a food processor or blender, combine milk, pudding mix and sour cream. Process 1 minute. Slice 1 banana; place slices in bottoms of 6 dessert dishes. Pour pudding mixture over sliced banana. Refrigerate 15 minutes or until ready to serve. To serve, slice remaining banana. Garnish each dish with banana slices. Makes 6 servings.

# Kahlúa Chocolate Mousse

*Your favorite liqueur can replace the Kahlúa.*

1 cup (6 oz.) semisweet chocolate pieces
2 eggs, separated
1/2 teaspoon vanilla extract
1/2 cup sugar

1 cup whipping cream
2 tablespoons Kahlúa or other liqueur
Orange peel

Melt chocolate in a double boiler over simmering water; remove from heat. Stir in egg yolks and vanilla; set aside. Beat egg whites in a small bowl until nearly stiff. Beat in 1/4 cup sugar until very stiff; set aside. In a medium bowl, whip cream until soft peaks form. Beat in 1/4 cup sugar and liqueur until very stiff. Fold chocolate mixture into whipped cream; gently fold in beaten egg whites. Pour mixture into a serving dish or dessert dishes. Chill in freezer until ready to serve. If longer than 45 minutes, chill in refrigerator. Cut orange peel in 3- to 4-inch-long strips, about 1/4-inch wide. Tie each strip in a knot. Garnish mousse with orange-peel knots, if desired. Makes 6 to 8 servings.

# Raspberry-Mallow Mousse

*For a special touch, top each serving with a spoonful of kirsch or garnish with grated chocolate.*

1 (10-oz.) pkg. frozen raspberries, thawed
1/2 lb. marshmallows (about 30)

1 cup whipping cream, whipped

Drain raspberries, reserving juice; set berries aside. Combine raspberry juice and marshmallows in a medium saucepan over low heat. Cook, stirring frequently, until marshmallows melt. Place in freezer to cool to room temperature, stirring occasionally. When marshmallow mixture reaches room temperature, fold in whipped cream and reserved berries. Spoon into 5 or 6 dessert dishes. Chill until ready to serve. Makes 5 or 6 servings.

# Quick Pots de Crème

*The height of chocolate desserts!*

1 cup (6 oz.) semisweet chocolate pieces
1 (14-oz.) can sweetened condensed milk
1 teaspoon rum extract

2 cups frozen whipped topping or
   whipped cream
Flaked coconut or shaved chocolate

In a medium saucepan, melt chocolate over low heat. Stir in condensed milk until smooth. Remove from heat; stir in rum extract. Cool in freezer 10 minutes. Then stir in whipped topping or cream. Pour into creme pots or dessert dishes. Chill in freezer until ready to serve. If longer than 45 minutes, chill in refrigerator. To serve, garnish with coconut or chocolate. Makes 8 (1/2-cup) servings.

**Tip**

*Whipping cream produces the most volume if cream, beaters and bowl are ice cold.*

**10**

# Hot-Fudge Sauce

*It's hard to find a chocolate sauce on the market that can match this for taste.*

1 (14-oz.) can sweetened condensed milk
1/2 cup brewed coffee
1 (7-oz.) jar marshmallow cream

2 cups (12 oz.) semisweet chocolate pieces
1 teaspoon vanilla extract

In a medium saucepan, combine all ingredients. Cook over medium heat, stirring frequently, until chocolate melts and is blended in completely. Serve over ice cream. Refrigerate any leftover sauce. To reheat, place in saucepan over low heat. Stir occasionally until warm and smooth. Makes 3-1/2 cups.

### Variation

**Grand Marnier Fudge Sauce:** Substitute 1/4 cup Grand Marnier or other orange liqueur and 1/4 cup milk for 1/2 cup coffee.

**20**

# Double-Chocolate Fudge

*Rich creamy fudge that takes minutes to make but tastes complicated.*

2 cups (12 oz.) semisweet chocolate pieces
1 cup (6 oz.) milk chocolate pieces
1 (14-oz.) can sweetened condensed milk

1 teaspoon vanilla extract
3/4 cup chopped walnuts

Butter an 8-inch-square pan; set aside. In a heavy saucepan, melt chocolate pieces over low heat; stir occasionally until smooth. Remove from heat; stir in condensed milk and vanilla. Beat vigorously until smooth and blended. Pour into buttered pan. Sprinkle walnuts over top. Chill in freezer 15 minutes. Cut into 1-inch squares. Makes 64 (1-inch) pieces.

**25**

# Rapid Rocky-Road Fudge

*Quick-to-fix fudge that keeps in the freezer up to three months.*

1 cup (6 oz.) semisweet chocolate pieces
1 cup (6 oz.) butterscotch-flavored pieces
1 (14-oz.) can sweetened condensed milk

1 teaspoon vanilla extract
1 cup chopped walnuts
1 cup marshmallows

Butter an 8-inch-square pan; set aside. In a heavy saucepan, melt chocolate and butterscotch pieces over low heat; stir occasionally until smooth. Remove from heat; stir in condensed milk and vanilla. Beat vigorously until smooth. Stir in walnuts and marshmallows. Pour into buttered pan. Chill in freezer 15 minutes. Cut into 1-inch squares. Makes 64 (1-inch) pieces.

## Tip

*Freezing walnuts and marshmallows before using helps speed setting of chocolate.*

# How to Make Peppermint-Ice-Cream Cake

1/Cut a 1/2-inch slice off top of cake; cut or scoop out inside, leaving a 1/2-inch-thick shell.

2/Spoon ice cream into cutout cake. Gently press with the back of the spoon to fill cake completely.

**10**

## Peppermint-Ice-Cream Cake

*English-toffee ice cream is also good in this cake.*

1 loaf-shape angel food cake
1 pint peppermint-stick ice cream,
   slightly softened

1 (12-oz.) can chocolate-fudge topping or
   Hot-Fudge Sauce, opposite

Cut off a 1/2-inch slice from top of cake. Cut or scoop out inside of cake, leaving a 1/2-inch-thick shell. Gently press ice cream into hollow cake. Replace top. Wrap with plastic wrap; freeze until ready to serve. To serve, cut into 1-inch-thick slices. Top with warm chocolate sauce. Makes 8 servings.

**15**

## Chocolate-Marshmallow Fondue

*Top a slice of angel food cake with this rich chocolate sauce.*

1 cup (6 oz.) semisweet chocolate pieces
1-1/2 cups miniature marshmallows

1 cup half and half
1 teaspoon vanilla extract

In a medium saucepan, combine chocolate, marshmallows and half and half. Cover and cook over low heat 10 minutes, stirring occasionally to blend. Remove from heat; stir until smooth. Add vanilla. Serve with fruit and angel-food-cake pieces for dipping. Or, serve warm or cold over ice cream. Makes 1-1/2 cups.

# Strawberry Grand Marnier Ice Cream

*Keep all ingredients on hand for this perfect impromptu dessert.*

1 cup whipping cream
1/2 cup sugar
2 tablespoons Grand Marnier or
   other orange liqueur

1 (20-oz.) bag frozen unsweetened whole
   strawberries

In a blender or food processor, combine cream, sugar and liqueur. Turn machine on and drop in frozen strawberries, 1 at a time. Process until strawberries are pureed and cream is frozen. Serve immediately in attractive stemmed glasses. Leftovers can be placed in a freezer container and frozen, but will be icy and not as smooth. Makes 4 to 6 servings.

# Blueberries & Grand Marnier Whipped Cream

*Use leftover whipped cream to top off a steaming cup of coffee.*

1 pint fresh blueberries
1 cup whipping cream
2 tablespoons Grand Marnier or
   other orange liqueur

2 tablespoons powdered sugar

Rinse blueberries in a strainer; remove any stems. Drain well. In a deep bowl, whip cream until soft peaks form. Add liqueur and sugar. Whip until cream is stiff but not dry. Spoon blueberries into 4 to 6 all-purpose wine glasses. Top with flavored whipped cream. Makes 4 to 6 servings.

# Sherry Sauce

*Serve over a compote of fresh fruit.*

1/4 cup butter or margarine
1 cup sugar
1/2 cup whipping cream

3 tablespoons dry sherry
1/2 teaspoon vanilla extract

In a small saucepan, melt butter or margarine with sugar. Stir in whipping cream, sherry and vanilla until blended. Serve warm or refrigerate until needed. Makes 1-1/2 cups.

# Spirited Cherry Topping

*Use this topping for ice cream or pound-cake slices.*

1 (21-oz.) can cherry-pie filling
2 tablespoons amaretto liqueur

1/4 cup whipping cream
2 tablespoons slivered almonds

In a small saucepan, combine all ingredients. Heat over medium heat until warm through. Makes 6 to 8 servings.

# Chocolate-Mint-Frosted Brownies

**30**

*Frosted brownies with the fastest frosting you'll ever make.*

2 oz. unsweetened chocolate
1/4 cup butter or margarine
2 eggs
1 cup sugar
2/3 cup all-purpose flour

1/4 teaspoon salt
1/2 teaspoon vanilla extract
1/4 teaspoon peppermint extract
16 round chocolate-mint candies

Preheat oven to 350F (175C). Grease an 8-inch-square baking pan; set aside. In a small bowl or saucepan, melt chocolate and butter or margarine; cool to room temperature. In a medium bowl, combine eggs and sugar. Stir in cooled chocolate mixture. Add flour, salt, vanilla and peppermint extract. Pour into greased pan. Bake 20 minutes. As soon as brownies are removed from oven, place chocolate candies evenly on top. Let stand 5 minutes. Then use a knife to swirl melted candies to frost brownies. Cut brownies into 2-inch squares. Makes 16 servings.

# Apple-Raisin Bars

**22**

*For a special treat, top these bars with a scoop of ice cream.*

1/2 cup vegetable shortening
1 cup packed brown sugar
1 egg
1/4 cup apple juice or milk
2 cups all-purpose flour
1/2 teaspoon ground nutmeg

1 teaspoon ground cinnamon
1/2 teaspoon ground cloves
1 cup finely chopped apple
1 cup raisins
1/2 cup chopped walnuts
Lemon Glaze, below

Preheat oven to 375F (190C). Grease an 8-inch-square baking pan; set aside. In a medium bowl, cream shortening and sugar. Blend in egg and apple juice or milk. Add flour, nutmeg, cinnamon and cloves; blend well. Stir in apple, raisins and walnuts. Spoon into greased pan. Bake 15 minutes. While baking, prepare Lemon Glaze. Cut baked mixture into 2-inch squares. Serve Lemon Glaze over hot bars. Makes 16 (2-inch) bars.

# Lemon Glaze

**4**

*Sifting powdered sugar results in a very smooth glaze.*

1-1/2 cups powdered sugar
1/4 cup fresh lemon juice

In a medium bowl, combine sugar and lemon juice; beat until smooth. Serve over hot Apple-Raisin Bars, above. Makes 3/4 cup.

 **Tip**

*Three medium apples are equal to about 1 pound. A medium apple yields about 1 cup peeled, sliced or diced fruit.*

# How to Make Chocolate Garnish

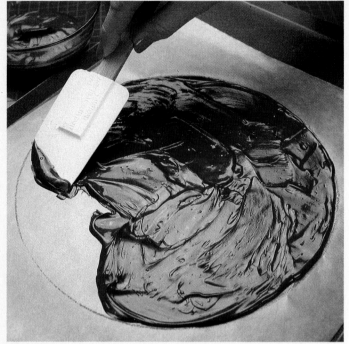

1/Spread melted chocolate mixture on waxed paper to fill the circle.

2/Lift chocolate wedges off with a spatula to prevent melting.

**10**

## Chocolate Garnish

*Use these to add a touch of elegance to any chocolate dessert.*

**3 oz. semisweet chocolate**
**1/2 teaspoon vanilla extract**

Draw a 9-inch circle on waxed paper. Melt chocolate in a small heavy saucepan over low heat. Stir in vanilla until mixture is smooth. Place waxed paper on a small baking sheet to keep flat. Spread mixture on waxed paper to fill circle. Refrigerate 10 minutes or until slightly firm. Cut into 8 wedges but do not separate pieces. Refrigerate until ready to serve. Invert chocolate circle on baking sheet. Gently peel off waxed paper. Lift chocolate wedges off with spatula to prevent melting. Serve as a base for dessert or stand on edge on top of wedge of cake for decoration. Makes 8 wedges.

**7**

## Chantilly Cream

*Serve this delicious cream over fresh berries or any fresh fruit.*

**1/2 cup whipping cream**                **3 tablespoons powdered sugar**
**1/2 cup dairy sour cream**              **1-1/2 teaspoons vanilla extract**

In a small bowl, whip cream until stiff. Add sour cream, sugar and vanilla; beat until smooth. This cream will keep up to 2 days in the refrigerator. Makes 1-1/2 cups.

# Beverages

For a meal prepared in 30 minutes or less, each dish has to play a special part and easily fit a preparation schedule. Often we forget how important a beverage is for flavor and color as well as for refreshment. The flavor should blend with or complement the meal. If the beverage will be served alone, such as a dessert coffee or afternoon refresher, it should have a distinct flavor and fit the overall mood.

Seek out a knowledgeable wine and liqueur dealer. He can often make suggestions as to a wine, beer or non-alcoholic beverage that would best complement your meal. A good suggestion for a non-alcoholic festive drink would be a sparkling grape juice. You might want to plan on serving two beverages, one with alcohol and one without, giving your guests a choice. Don't forget about serving ice water. It's welcome at any meal.

For breakfast, brunch or lunch, there is a wide range of beverages to choose from. Sweeter drinks seem more appropriate here than at dinner. Light meals can accommodate a fruit-juice combination such as Spiced Grape Juice or a flavored tea.

For after-dinner drinks or as a dessert, flavored and liqueured coffees add elegance. A most impressive and quick way to present plain or flavored coffee is to set out a tray of seasonings. Include small bowls of grated orange or lemon peel, mini chocolate pieces, fresh cream and colored sugar. Allow guests to serve themselves. Colored rock-type sugar along with special flavored decaffeinated coffee and tea are now widely available. An easy way to remember which guests are drinking decaffeinated drinks is to slip a small doily under those cups for uncomplicated refilling.

A large selection of attractive yet inexpensive glassware and mugs is available today. Serve beverages in lovely inexpensive glasses and don't worry as you would with expensive crystal. Determine the number of guests and types of drinks you will most often serve before buying glassware. Many glasses are multi-purpose. An all-purpose goblet can double as a parfait glass.

An old-fashioned glass could serve juice for breakfast, a cold soup for lunch and an Old Fashioned for evening cocktails. Mugs are excellent for coffee or tea, cocoa or soup. You can rarely have too many glasses.

Having drinks at the correct serving temperature is as important as the flavor. Keep hot drinks refilled. Place the pitcher over a candlewarmer, on the stove or in the microwave. If you reheat drinks in the microwave, be sure cups do not have gold, silver or metallic trim. For cold drinks, place glasses in the freezer ahead of time for a frosty appearance. Be sure to make extra ice available for guests to refill glasses.

When deciding on a beverage to serve, it's easy to think only in terms of Chablis or Burgundy for a wine, or milk, coffee or tea. With a little imagination, you can turn these standards into stars. Use this interesting selection of fun drinks to add a new dimension to any meal.☙

---

## Breakfast Date Shake

*For an afternoon treat, add a scoop of vanilla ice cream.*

**1 egg**
**4 pitted dates, cut in quarters**

**1 cup milk**
**Ground nutmeg**

Process egg in a blender until frothy. Add dates and milk; process 30 seconds. Dates should be finely chopped. Pour into a glass; sprinkle nutmeg over top. Makes 1 serving.

## Breakfast Yogurt Shake

*The perfect early morning wake-up beverage.*

**1 cup apricot-pineapple yogurt (8 oz.)**
**2 cups apricot nectar, chilled**

In a blender, combine yogurt and nectar; process until smooth. Pour into glasses to serve. Makes 2 servings.

**Variation**

Substitute any flavor yogurt with a complementary juice.

## Orange Eye-Opener Drink

*Breakfast in a glass!*

**1 pint orange juice (2 cups)**
**2 eggs**
**1 cup milk**

**1/4 cup wheat germ**
**2 tablespoons honey**
**4 ice cubes**

Combine all ingredients in a blender. Process at high speed until smooth. Makes 2 servings.

# Orange Breakfast Tea

*For a cool afternoon drink, serve over ice.*

3 cups boiling water
1 tablespoon tea leaves
1/3 cup sugar

1 (6-oz.) can frozen-orange-juice concentrate,
   reconstituted

In a large teapot, pour boiling water over tea leaves; steep 5 minutes. Strain into a large saucepan. Add sugar and orange juice. Heat to desired serving temperature. Pour into mugs. Makes 4 to 6 servings.

# Fresh-Fruit Soda

*Use your imagination and a variety of fresh fruit for a range of flavors.*

2 cups fresh pineapple chunks
1 large peach, cut into chunks
10 strawberries

1/4 cup or more sugar
Cracked ice
1 qt. club soda, chilled

In a blender, combine pineapple, peach, 6 strawberries and 1/4 cup sugar; process until liquified. Add additional sugar to taste. Fill 4 glasses with cracked ice. Pour fruit mixture over ice in glasses to about 1/2 full; add club soda to fill glasses. Stir gently. Garnish each with a whole strawberry. Makes 4 servings.

# Pink Sun

*Two favorites, orange juice and strawberries, blended into a tasty drink.*

1 cup orange juice
1/2 cup strawberries, sliced

4 ice cubes

In a blender, combine orange juice and strawberries. With blender running, drop in ice cubes, 1 at a time, until crushed. Makes 1 serving.

# Spiced Grape Juice

*A grown-up version of grape juice.*

1 qt. water (4 cups)
4 teaspoons tea leaves
3/4 cup sugar
1/2 cup fresh lemon juice

2 (2-inch) cinnamon sticks
5 whole cloves
3 cups grape juice
Ice cubes

In a small saucepan, bring 1 cup water to a boil; remove from heat. Add tea leaves, sugar, lemon juice, cinnamon sticks and cloves. Cover and steep 10 minutes. Strain into a pitcher; add remaining water and grape juice. Serve over ice. Makes 2 quarts.

# Citrus Frappé

*Citrus flavors are always refreshing.*

1 (6-oz.) can frozen-orange-juice
   concentrate
1 cup grapefruit juice
1/4 cup fresh lemon juice

1 egg white
3 tablespoons powdered sugar
2 cups cracked ice

Place orange-juice concentrate, grapefruit juice, lemon juice, egg white and powdered sugar in a blender or food processor. Process until foamy, about 1 minute. Gradually add ice, processing until mixture is smooth. Serve immediately. Makes 4 servings.

# Icy Orange Shake

*Cool and refreshing best describes this drink.*

1 cup orange sherbet
1 pint orange juice (2 cups)

In a blender, process sherbet and orange juice until smooth. Serve immediately. Makes 2 servings.

**Variations**

**Icy Pineapple Shake:** Substitute pineapple sherbet and pineapple juice in the same amounts.
**Icy Lime Shake:** Substitute lime sherbet and limeade in the same amounts.
**Icy Lemon Shake:** Substitute lemon sherbet and lemonade in the same amounts.

# Cranberry-Orange Cooler

*Just pour and drink.*

1 pint cranberry juice (2 cups)
1 pint orange juice (2 cups)
Ice cubes

4 mint sprigs
4 orange slices

In a medium pitcher, combine cranberry juice and orange juice. Serve over ice. Garnish with mint sprigs and orange slices. Makes 4 servings.

# Lemonade Rosé     *Photo on pages 78, 79*

*Grown-up lemonade at last.*

1 (6-oz.) can frozen-lemonade concentrate,
   reconstituted
1 (4/5-qt.) bottle rosé, chilled

Sugar, if desired
Ice cubes

In a large pitcher, blend lemonade and rosé. Add sugar to taste. Serve over ice. Makes 5 to 6 servings.

# How to Make Frosty Grapefruit Julep

1/In a medium bowl, combine mint and sugar; mash with a fork.

2/Serve over ice cubes. Garnish each serving with a mint sprig.

**10**

## Frosty Grapefruit Julep

*Fresh mint is the similar ingredient between this drink and the original mint julep.*

1 (6-oz.) can frozen-grapefruit-juice
   concentrate, reconstituted
1 cup snipped fresh mint leaves
1 cup sugar

1/2 cup lime juice
2 (7-oz.) bottles sparkling water
Ice cubes
Mint sprigs

In a medium saucepan, bring 2 cups grapefruit juice to a boil. In a medium bowl, combine snipped mint and sugar; mash with a fork. Pour hot juice over mint mixture. Cool slightly; strain juice. Discard mint. Add remaining grapefruit juice and lime juice to strained juice. Refrigerate. To serve, add sparkling water. Serve over ice. Garnish each serving with a mint sprig. Makes 8 servings.

## Tip

*For an elegant touch, frost glasses by dipping rims lightly in grapefruit juice, then in sugar.*

# Chocolate-Cream Soda

*Sodas are as refreshing as milk shakes, but with fewer calories.*

**1/4 cup whipping cream**
**2 tablespoons chocolate syrup**

**Club soda, chilled**

In a tall glass, combine whipping cream and chocolate syrup. Fill glass with club soda. Makes 1 serving.

**Variation**

Fill glass 1/2 full with club soda; blend in chocolate syrup. Add 1 scoop vanilla or chocolate ice cream. Fill glass to top with club soda.

# Chocolate-Galliano Shake

*Invent a new drink—substitute your own favorite liqueur combination.*

**1 pint chocolate ice cream**
**3 tablespoons Galliano liqueur**

**3 tablespoons crème de cacao liqueur**

Spoon ice cream into a blender; add liqueurs. Process until smooth. Pour into 2 glasses. Serve with a spoon. Makes 2 servings.

# Hot Buttered-Rum Cider

*There is no substitute for real butter in this recipe.*

**1 cup vanilla ice cream**
**1/4 cup butter**
**3/4 cup packed brown sugar**
**1/4 teaspoon ground nutmeg**
**1/2 teaspoon ground cinnamon**

**1 cup dark rum**
**1-1/2 qts. apple cider or strong coffee,**
  **heated (6 cups)**
**8 (3-inch) cinnamon sticks**

In a mixer or food processor, blend ice cream, butter, brown sugar, nutmeg and ground cinnamon until smooth. Place mixture in freezer until ready to use. To serve, spoon 2 tablespoons ice-cream mixture into each of 8 mugs. Add 2 tablespoons rum to each mug. Fill each mug with hot cider or coffee. Garnish with cinnamon sticks. Makes 8 servings.

# Sherry-Eggnog Toddy

*Perfect to serve at a holiday gathering.*

**1 qt. eggnog (4 cups)**
**1 cup milk**
**3/4 cup dry sherry or rum**

**1/4 teaspoon ground nutmeg**
**Cinnamon sticks**

In a medium saucepan, combine eggnog, milk, sherry or rum and nutmeg. Bring to a simmer over low heat; do not boil. Serve hot with a cinnamon stick in each cup. Makes 8 servings.

**7**

# Peaches in Champagne

*An elegant beverage for afternoon entertaining.*

**2 medium peaches**
**1 bottle champagne, chilled**

For easy peeling, drop peaches in boiling water 15 to 30 seconds; then plunge into cold water. Peel and slice peaches; divide evenly among 4 champagne or all-purpose wine glasses. Pour champagne slowly into peach-filled glasses; be careful to prevent bubbling over. Serve with small forks. Glasses may be refilled with champagne before eating the peaches. Makes 4 servings.

**5**

# Sherry Shrub

*Refrigerate up to four days, if you have any leftovers.*

**1 (4/5-qt.) bottle dry sherry**          **Juice of 2 lemons**
**1 (6-oz.) can frozen-lemonade concentrate,**   **Ice cubes**
  **reconstituted**

Combine sherry, lemonade and lemon juice in a large pitcher. Serve over ice. Makes 5 to 6 servings.

**5**

# Margarita-Wine Punch

*Let guests serve themselves; then you'll be free to visit.*

**1 (1.5 liter) bottle margarita mix**       **Lime wedges**
**1 (1.5 liter) bottle white chablis**       **Salt**

In a 1-gallon punch bowl, combine margarita mix and chablis. Add ice or serve with a bucket of ice on the side. Place a bowl of lime wedges and a saucer of salt near the punch bowl. Guests may rub the rim of their glasses with lime; then dip in salt, if desired. Makes 3-1/2 quarts.

**15**

# Hot Williamsburg Punch

*When cooler fall temperatures arrive, serve this warm drink.*

**1 orange**                          **1 teaspoon ground nutmeg**
**1 qt. apple cider (4 cups)**             **6 whole cloves**
**1/4 cup lemon juice**                  **Additional cinnamon sticks, if desired**
**3 (3-inch) cinnamon sticks**

Using a paring knife, slice off colored peel from orange. In a medium saucepan, simmer orange peel, cider, lemon juice, 3 cinnamon sticks, nutmeg and cloves 10 minutes. Remove and discard spices and orange peel. Serve hot. Garnish each cup with a cinnamon stick, if desired. Makes 8 servings.

# Cocoa-Almond Café

*Perfect finale to a fine dinner.*

2 tablespoons unsweetened cocoa powder
1/4 cup sugar
2 tablespoons instant-coffee granules
1 qt. milk (4 cups)

1/2 cup whipping cream
2 tablespoons powdered sugar
1/2 teaspoon almond extract

In a medium saucepan, combine cocoa powder, sugar, coffee granules and milk. Warm over low heat to desired serving temperature; do not boil. Meanwhile, in a small bowl, whip cream until soft peaks form. Beat in powdered sugar and almond extract. Pour hot coffee mixture into cups. Garnish with whipped-cream mixture. Makes 4 to 6 servings.

# Bavarian Coffee

*A perfect warm, cozy drink to brighten up a cloudy day.*

1/2 cup (3 oz.) semisweet chocolate pieces
2 teaspoons instant-coffee granules

1 pint hot milk (2 cups)
Whipped cream

In a blender or food processor, combine chocolate pieces and coffee granules. Add milk; process until smooth. Pour into mugs. Top with whipped cream. Makes 2 servings.

# Spiked Mocha

*An adult version of a childhood favorite.*

1/4 cup unsweetened cocoa powder
1/4 cup sugar
1/4 cup strong black coffee or
   1/4 teaspoon instant-coffee granules and
   1/4 cup water
4 (2" x 1/4") strips fresh orange peel,
   colored part only

1 qt. milk (4 cups)
1/3 cup rum or crème de cacao liqueur,
   if desired
Grated orange peel

In a medium saucepan, combine cocoa powder, sugar, and coffee or coffee granules and water; blend well. Add orange-peel strips and milk. Warm over medium-low heat to desired serving temperature. Stir in rum or crème de cacao, if desired. Pour into mugs. Garnish with grated peel. Makes 4 servings.

# Amaretto Tea

*Amaretto is an almond-flavor liqueur.*

3/4 cup strong hot tea
2 tablespoons amaretto liqueur

Whipped cream

Pour hot tea into an 8-ounce glass or mug. Stir in liqueur. Top with a dollop of whipped cream. Makes 1 serving.

# Delicious Coffee Recipes

**Café Olé**
1 cup fresh hot coffee
1 tablespoon chocolate syrup
Cream
1 teaspoon sugar
Sprinkle of ground nutmeg and cinnamon

**Café Borgia**
Equal parts hot coffee and hot chocolate topped with whipped cream and grated orange peel.

**Café au Lait**
Equal portions of hot coffee and hot milk poured in at the same time.

**Cappucino**
Equal portions of hot coffee and hot milk topped with a sprinkle of powdered cocoa.

**Irish Coffee**
1 cup fresh hot coffee
2 teaspoons sugar
1 oz. Irish whiskey
Top with whipped cream

**Café Royal**
1 cup fresh hot coffee
1 oz. Cognac

# Coffee Buffet

Assemble a large tray with all or some of the ingredients listed. Allow your guests to create their favorite coffee combination.

Cinnamon sticks
Peppermint sticks
Rock sugar swizzle sticks
Lemon-peel strips
Grated orange peel
Hot milk

Miniature chocolate pieces
Sugar cubes
Colored sugar granules
Whole cloves
Powdered cocoa in a shaker
Whipped cream

Spirits & liqueurs—add 1 oz. per coffee cup

Amaretto
Galliano
Brandy
Cognac
Irish whiskey

Rum
Cointreau
Kahlúa
Crème de cacao

# Tips for Making a Perfect Cup of Coffee

• Select your favorite coffee. Grind it yourself or have it ground for you. Be sure the grind is correct for the type of coffee maker you use.
• Measure coffee and water carefully, using 1 tablespoon coffee per 3/4 cup water. For a weaker brew, add hot water after coffee is brewed.
• Use fresh cold water. If your tap water has an off taste, use bottled water.
• For the best flavor, serve coffee immediately after it is brewed. Coffee can be kept warm for up to 1 hour, if necessary.
• Ground coffee should be stored in an airtight container. Purchase only what you can use in 1 week. If longer storage is needed for ground coffee, refrigerate it or freeze for up to 2 months. Unground coffee beans can be stored in the freezer for 3 to 6 months.

# Index

8.426903863521